TRUTH

G000096099

"For now we see through a glass, darkly;
but then face to face: now I know in part;
but then shall I know even as also I am
known."

1 Corinthians. X111. 12

This book is dedicated to God, and his helpers on Earth.

TRUTH IS VEILED

A Practical Guide to
Life After Death

by

Peter Cowlin

Foreword
by
Denys Kelsey

Edited by
Michael and June Cowlin

Cover Art by Digby Curtis
Illustrated by Mark Farmer

SYNTHESIS PUBLISHING

British Library Cataloguing in Publication Data

Cowlin, P.
    Truth is Veiled: a practical guide to life after death
    I. Title
    133.9013

ISBN 0951807404

SYNTHESIS PUBLISHING
Portelet, Binstead Hall,
Binstead, Isle of Wight, UK.

Printed in the United Kingdom by
Billing & Sons Ltd, Worcester

Distributed by
Lifeworks, London
(*Orders:* Tel. 081–393 9689)

Disclaimer

This work does not claim to be the only true view of Life after Death. It is the vision of one Being, lately returned from Earth to the Spirit World, and rapidly broadening the scope of his consciousness to report what he has found from his own experience.

This book is not fiction, nor does it pretend to be a literary 'work of art'.

We are all climbing the same mountain towards the Divine light, but perhaps on different faces of the slope. Thus the view seen through one person's eyes may be very different to the view of another person on the opposite side of the mountain, and at a different height.

Let us not dispute which view is the truth. All may be equally valid!

We, the editors, hope this work will be some guide to those intent on climbing from the lower slopes of our mountain, and unsure of their own path.

On some scripts, names have been changed to protect relatives.

Acknowledgements

In writing this book, the editors would like to acknowledge with gratitude the help received from:

Mr D.B.Greaterex, for reading the manuscript and providing valuable comments and helpful criticisms.

Dr. Denys Kelsey for writing a foreword to the book.

Dr. D.M.A.Leggett, for encouraging comments on the book.

Mr Paul Beard, for permission to refer to his writing in general and for his encouragement and the very considerable interest he has taken in this work.

Our grateful thanks to all those other people who have made suggestions and offered helpful criticisms.

Michael and June Cowlin
February 1991

Table of Contents

Foreword by *Denys Kelsey*

M.B. B.Chir. M.R.C.P.

I believe this book is indeed a record of communications occurring mediumistically between June and Michael Cowlin, and their adopted son Peter, who left his physical body in 1987, aged seventeen following shortly after a motorcycle accident.

I base this belief on my experience that under Hypnotic Regression patients are able to relive, not only events occurring in the womb, and at conception, but can also recall earlier lifetimes. I have long been convinced that the Non-Physical component (*the spirit*) of a human being has a long history of lifetimes on this planet. Reincarnation is a cornerstone of the philosophical basis of my work. It was for this reason that I came to see Peter professionally. Some of his behaviour could indeed have had origins in an earlier incarnation—as do so many problems that mankind faces.

Much in this book supports information I myself was given during a brief period with a mediumistic faculty and which I have also heard from patients I have treated.

How does one know one is not misleading oneself? Peter discusses this possibility sensibly: *each reader must ultimately decide for himself.* I think it would have required a novelist of high calibre to have written the book out of his own head. I intend no discourtesy when I say I do not feel Peter's parents to be such novelists. Intuitively, I sense the communications have the ring of truth.

Peter's scripts are his effort to convince people, who happen currently to be in a physical body, that the Earth is a *school for spiritual development* and death a *return to one's real home.* There one can also continue to develop. Though the theme of 'freewill' runs throughout this book, there is no pressure, the choice is yours:

"You don't suddenly become wiser because you have died".

These communications do not purport to come from an advanced sage, but from an ordinary teenager (this time round anyway). Peter himself recognises that in terms of his spiritual evolution he still has a very long way to go. This I think is partly what makes this book such a persuasive and valuable document.

After reading this book, I think anyone who shares my view of its validity will have very much less to fear of the process of dying and of what we call 'death'. You will no longer feel that death is a permanent parting from loved ones. You will at least have less doubt about the reality of reincarnation.

In addition to this you will absorb a sense of purpose, not merely of each lifetime, but of your very existence.

This book left me with the hope that we may look forward, not only to future instalments of Peter's activities and evolution 'upstairs', but to a time when we may all accept that death is but a transition, a doorway, through which the truth of a greater life may be revealed.

Dr. Denys Kelsey is an eminent Psychiatrist of many years standing, specialising in regression and hypno-analysis, and is author with Joan Grant of the book "Many Lifetimes".

About This Book

Some people on picking up this book may perhaps recoil in horror at information received from 'beyond the grave'.

Others may be sufficiently intrigued to read further, and perhaps learn more about:

— Why are we alive on Earth? What is the purpose of our lives? What awaits us when we finally die, as we all must eventually?

They will no longer fear Death, and may perhaps re-order their lives to a more positive purpose.

These people's clearer vision will be the 'raison d'etre' for Peter's efforts in passing back information for this book.

Read it like a Guide Book

This book is divided into two parts:

PART 1 — Living through a death experience, what is it like?

This part describes how Peter "did it his own way...", and describes how he experienced dying and what lay beyond. These scripts are classified by 'topic' and cover a broad spectrum of experiences of how life can continue and what kind of 'environment' we may expect.

This part can be read straight through to gain a general impression of discarnate life, or used as a reference book for ideas concerning specific topics as they occur to you.

One should remember that this is Peter's experience—at a particular stage of his own development—and details may vary to some extent according to another individual's past life and experience (as does one's viewpoint on Earth).

PART 2 — Reviewing Past Lives, Learning by experience

This part consists of communications from other people who have passed beyond the veil to support the main message of this book:

That of understanding the purpose of life, and the role played by Serial Existences or reincarnation. Many lifetimes provide a means by which experiences enable the development of the Spirit to occur, the ultimate aim being union with God.

Many people are totally unprepared for the transition from physical existence, and a number of ordinary folk have given their own initial experiences and reactions. They have endeavoured to prepare people for continuation of consciousness after death.

A list of topics is provided at the front of each chapter.
A Glossary and general index is also provided to help
you find your way around.

Learning From Life

The Reader may observe evidence of Peter's maturing consciousness in the complexities of some of the scripts; in particular we recommend you read the Introductions and the Summaries at the end of each chapter which were given towards the later part of the period covered by this book.

Peter emphasises the lessons he feels he has learned through his own past life experiences, and he summarises these in Chapter 9. He also assesses his recent life as Peter at the end of that chapter. The aspects of character he now feels he has mastered from within are quoted in the final paragraph of that summary.

How This Book Was Compiled

The true author of this book is Peter, our dead son. We, his parents, have acted as the receivers, compilers, and editors. The information given is from Peter, with minimum input from ourselves.

We selected from more than a thousand scripts recorded by us in the preceding two and a half years those scripts we thought to be of wide enough interest, and have classified them. These have been vetted by Peter. Introductions to the sections of the book, and summaries at the end of sections, were with a few exceptions, dictated by Peter. Early on in our conversations, Peter had indicated that he wanted to write a book to carry to those on Earth, firstly, the message that 'Death', in the way most people in the Western World regard it, does not exist—there is no oblivion of the person. Though the physical body is destroyed, the non-material parts of the Being: the Personality, Soul, and Spirit, live on. Indeed, the Personality is, initially, little changed from that known on Earth, and to most 'discarnates', change after death occurs, but slowly.

Secondly, Peter wants to show to those now incarnate the reason for their lives on Earth, and how they should be living *to reap maximum benefit for the development of their Spirit.* Life on Earth is a school for such development, though too often this is not appreciated by those living. Peter illustrates the natural law of sequential lives, known commonly as "Reincarnation", through reference to his own past lives on Earth, and those of some of his friends and relatives. He shows how over many, many lifetimes undesirable characteristics in the Personality are overcome, and the Spirit slowly develops towards a higher level of existence, towards the Divine light.

We hope that the truths of which Peter wants to remind mankind will be well received and acted upon quickly: all the information has been available for hundreds of years to those who seek the truth. The Earth is now very polluted, and those passing back to Spirit may find very difficult conditions when they next incarnate. Some people talk about saving the Earth for the coming generations; these generations may include such people themselves!

The work of producing this book has taken over and transformed our lives. We feel very privileged to have been able to cooperate with our son in this task.

INTRODUCTION

1 — *by Michael and June Cowlin*

Peter would have been 18 on 7th March 1987. He was happiest out-of-doors. He had delighted in the new found freedom that his 100 cc Suzuki motorbike had given him since the previous Autumn, and in six months had travelled almost 7000 miles. He was well acquainted with it's handling in all kinds of inclement weather.

Monday 16th February 1987 had been a happy day. Peter lived near his school at Kings Langley, and that afternoon he had acquired components for building twin stereo speaker units, his choice for an individual school project. At 11.00 p.m. he was preparing for bed, when outside a familiar toot on the horn of a car told him a friend was passing. He remembered he wanted to talk urgently. Could it not have waited till the morning?

"Just going out", he announced to his 'alter Mum'. She did not hear him start the engine, and thought he was talking outside. Unaware of the events that followed, the household slept till morning.

Peter's parents were rung by Reading Police at 1.00 a.m. He had been involved in a motorcycle accident, and was in Watford Hospital. The weather had been cold, but dry, with good visibility. Traversing a familiar straight mile of dual carriageway he had failed to remember a minor road crossing. He saw too late the traffic lights at red; he could not stop in time and hit the rear of a car crossing slowly in his path.

"He sustained a moderate to severe head injury", said Watford Hospital. He was unconscious, and being moved to a London Head Injury unit for assessment. His parents felt numb, and helpless. They were advised his life was not in danger, and there was no need to panic. At 5 a.m. he was on his way back to Watford Hospital, having been found to need emergency surgery for a ruptured spleen: there were no obvious head complications. By 10 a.m. he had survived a forty mile round trip, followed by surgery, and was in "I.T.U." in good hands, and as well as could be expected.

A Healer friend spent several hours with him that evening, and in the anxious days that followed she passed energy into his battered body. By Friday he was off the ventilator, and although not speaking, withdrew his hand from his mother's and gave the thumbs-up sign, followed by a firm hand shake. She was full of hope.

He was moved to the orthopaedic ward and with help began to walk. Medical staff seemed satisfied with his progress. He read and reread the many 'get well' cards from friends. He spoke a few words, and wrote a few more. He constantly gazed at the main light in the ward, and absent mindedly fingered the bulb of the anglepoise over his bed until the nurse moved it away for safety.

Visitors came and went, but got little verbal response from Peter. This became a cause of concern for his family, but nursing staff said he had spoken, and his responses when made were logical. He seemed relaxed.

In retrospect, it seems Peter could not forget the 'beings of light' who had said they would return for him. (*See Post Accident scripts 30.3 87 and 18.7.88, Chapter 1*).

Towards the end of the week he seemed increasingly pre-occupied, and would smile as though in response to a conversation with other folk, of whom those by his bed were unaware.

On Saturday 28th February '87, the medical team did a ward round in the afternoon, and seemed satisfied with his progress. He was taken off frequent monitoring.

"He will be alright", his mother was told. "He's fully conscious now."

Peter listened, his gaze seemed incredulous, it was as if he knew differently. A few hours later his temperature rose and he began to vomit. The Cardiac Arrest team were called, but in a space of minutes, Peter was gone. His mother and a teacher with her were helpless onlookers to this drama which had descended without warning on what had started as a happy afternoon. They were stunned, as was everyone who was shortly to hear the news. Cerebral Oedema was the official cause of death, no fractured skull, no internal bleeding. It seemed inconceivable!

INTRODUCTION

For Peter's father his philosophy of Healing told him that it is only the physical body that suffers destruction at death, the Soul and Spirit live on. He was convinced that the essential Peter was near them still. The 'etheric field', though faint was still present four days after death, and feeling it made identification less traumatic than it might otherwise have been. For the time being he could detach himself emotionally from the event. The physical loss was a long term ache yet to be fully felt.

On the 9th March '87 the sun shone brightly, as though to try to give some cheer to Peter's family and many friends who gathered for the Cremation Service. Friends from his old school; friends, staff, and parents from the Rudolph Steiner schools in Kent, and at Kings Langley, where he was still a pupil were there, as were family friends, who had known Peter well, and others who had only met him briefly. A choir from his current school sang, a horn solo was played by a class friend. The Chapel was full, it seemed to vibrate with light, as the service, based on Rudolph Steiner's philosophy, was led by a member of the Christian Community. Several people commented that it seemed as though Peter filled the building. Other clairvoyant members of the congregation were aware of his presence. In the midst of sadness there was an uplifting atmosphere.

As Peter's family began to consider their loss it appeared from the numerous letters of condolence received that it would be a loss felt by very many others who had grown to know and love the kindly, helpful, golden haired lad with the mischievous grin.

This golden haired babe had joined the Cowlin family in August 1969. He was six months old, a long awaited son, by adoption. He developed quickly, and showed independence and self-determination from an early age.

"Don't need nappy", he announced one evening, and sure enough he knew! Things were already happening his way Viz: Peter's script 14.9.89:

> "I feel you should try to give a picture of the sort of difficult situations that arose in my childhood in terms of complying with recognised standards. A good comparison with (sister) Anne could be made. I seldom did what was expected of a normal child; she seldom did what was not the acceptable behaviour of her peers. I just want you to bring out the difference—that both can lead to a successful growth

in terms of personal development. I feel that knowledge of this is important. We all have our route to follow. Our aims have their foundation in the same need which is to develop desirable characteristics".

Through the faculty of 'clairaudience' or telepathy, which had developed some ten years earlier, Peter's father distinctly heard Peter speak to him on a number of occasions following his death. Peter had even jokingly suggested that "The Entertainer", a favourite with him, be included in the service to lighten the atmosphere. But, dare one trust what one hears when the involvement is so personal?

It was through a family friend, a trance medium, that other messages came, and with whom a regular circle was formed in August '87. Following which, with renewed confidence in what was actually happening, Peter's father sat each morning at 6 a.m., and after a brief meditation found that almost at once Peter and he were in contact. This was the start of regular communications of which a small portion of the scripts are quoted in the following pages.

In January 1988, June Cowlin also started to receive direct communication with Peter (re. Introduction to Part 2).

INTRODUCTION

2 — *by Peter Cowlin*

Sept./Oct. 1989

"I completely forgot the impact my departure from Earth would have. Aberration became a major factor in my commitment to communication. I had an idea that my family would know that we all survive death and would convene our original Plan with alacrity. You see we had decided long ago what we needed to master. I subconsciously knew from an early age that I should not be long on Earth, but from here I could immediately see that my family had completely forgotten any such arrangement.

I saw with amazement initially how upset they were, and in the early days of my death I tried to make my presence felt. Dad picked up the vibration, but doubted that a great deal was actually me. Mum could not sense my presence, and felt desperately lacking in consolation.

I began to feel confused by the situation, and wondered why I had such difficulty in reassuring the appropriate people of my presence. I felt I had failed by not discussing my actual plan, to which all had at one time consented. You must understand I had no idea what hard work it would be to convince my family that I actually existed, and that we all had work to do for the sake of the Earth's future well being.

I always tended to take on tasks beyond my capacity, not really to impress others, but because I have difficulty in assessing the immensity of my ideas, or perhaps I underestimate the necessary ground work. I knew I wanted to succeed. I realised I had much spade work to do and found the initial stages made inroads into my actual capacity for sticking it out.

My parents conscientiously pressed on through much heart searching and questioning. I had got to get to the stage which I anticipated would be the constructive one by continually hammering home,

"Death does not exist!"

Like most youngsters I had a propensity to get into mischief. Like most adults, my parents were concerned lest my behaviour should lead me into unacceptable diversions, and an answer to my lazy ways of pursuing intellectual learning was frequently sought.

INTRODUCTION

An answer too was sought for my propensity to take off from school 'at the drop of a hat'. I was often missing at teatime, or else having to be retrieved when I should have been home and preparing for bed. In later teenage years it was not so much concern for possible danger that I might be in, but rather for what mischief I might try to create.

However, not even my family were in a very knowledgeable position when my finale occurred. I am deliberately calling it this because, when I had experienced the consequences of my actions, I knew I wanted to abandon such behaviour once and for all.

"Ah", you will say. "He got into real trouble. Must have been punished, and didn't much like it!"

How reassuring this is.

"We need tough punishment, and then crime will cease...", you may say.

How very far from making the right assumption you could be. This will perhaps become clearer as you make some effort to consider my words.

I was not a criminal at heart. I wanted little more than to explore new concepts. The things available on Earth that had not been around when I last lived on Earth were all of immense interest to me: Television sets, Motor cars, mechanical operations of all kinds—not only to admire but to handle personally.

Also I could never understand why I was expected to devote so much energy to trying to explain on paper all I perceived. I felt a great need to enjoy all the Earth had to offer, because, from my inner being I knew my spell on Earth would be short.

"How?", you may ask?

Please do not dismiss this contentious statement. I question whether an element of recognition of this truth may already have been appreciated. Have none of you been tempted to almost concede that a particular course of events in your life is inescapable? It is of this depth of experience that I speak.

I only want to draw your attention to the fact that we act according to our *inner understanding* of life's pattern, not totally for reasons of fighting society's norm, but because of the need to go through certain experiences in order to learn how to survive, or to try to understand how others survive.

Very often we need to question our understanding of knowledge which we have acquired in our past lives, because little can be understood without relevant practical experience. We subject ourselves to behaviour which gives first hand irrefutable knowledge of how people both feel and react in a given situation. Unless one submits to an unlawful action one can never know how it's effect is actually thought through, or how another sees the situation. In your realisation comes the ability to forgive those who transgress in Society's eyes.

When you are in a position of condemning other's actions, please give a little thought to ignorance making the cost high for many endeavouring to tread the path of enlightenment. It could be made clear that only those who experience will make progress, and then evidence of learning might carry more weight, and the demand for punishment might get less support. A hard life often holds more positive spiritual development, than one whose participant is described as a 'Pillar of society'.

Have you any concept of life beyond death? Have you a preconceived idea of how things will be? Do you imagine that oblivion is the dominating fact for recognition?

Must oblivion be the order of things, or do you adhere to the vision of God on his throne receiving his children and allocating a place in Heaven for those who have tried to follow his commandments?

I wonder what are your hopes for the future. Must you denigrate those who indulge their Earthly appetites? Are you fearful of admitting both your desires, and your failures, least of all the indiscretions which partially colour the cloak you wear when greeting the ordinary world of material existence?

Just stop a moment to contemplate how you will drape fresh raiments upon your being as you advance, rested and hopeful before God's throne. Apparently life has left you momentarily vulnerable to being misunderstood. The 'robe' is showing signs of several skirmishes with a variety of different risque undertakings having caused severe damage to it's fabric.

I feel this to be a severe, indeed punishing, load to shoulder. May be good only for keeping some on the straight and narrow path for part of life's way. Perhaps one could be forgiven for wondering if oblivion could make for greater peace of mind, and present less inner turmoil to it's adherents.

I hope the descriptions that are made in the following pages are of some help in dispelling fear about Death to whichever camp you belong. I trust a number of you may feel inspired to venture further into the real world that can open to you, if you accept that communication and guidance *can* emanate from a discarnate source. A new source of hope and inspiration can operate in your life if you will allow such access to your mind. This implies a readiness to acknowledge, not oppose, an equal partnership of minds functioning in unison.

For unison to be operative, the order of the day must be openness and equality. But do not confuse this with a state of bombastic inferiority!"

Formative Years

"Like so many, I have happy memories of childhood days. They seemed both carefree and fun. One does not at the time see meaning in the ups and downs, that good times and difficult ones both have a place in the scheme of things. A great deal of heartache would be saved if parents understood that life actually is the stepping stone on the road to eternity.

What becomes of us eventually will be so—as the result of our own efforts. Sometimes we fail and our progress is halted. Sometimes we are interrupted by circumstances beyond our control. But, whatever happens it is both painless, and at the same time, constructive.

I believe I can already sense some gloom and protest as these words are read. But, I repeat, no 'pain' is experienced by the Eternal Spirit, which is sallying forth on it's next project, once it has acknowledged it's true home. No real distress is experienced either; disappointment often, when failure to complete the plan of one's life is realised.

I feel some good account of boyhood development should contain the description of a life well spent, and also one about tribulations. I describe the former as 'a rascal risen from the ashes'. and the latter as 'a fallen angel whose wings have not grown'."

INTRODUCTION

Learning From Experience

"Knowledge of life is not implicit in the growing years of a child. 'Knowledge' is given out by children's therapists and child welfare groups about physical well being and personality, as well as intellectual development. But, in the present age, the knowledge that was freely available in the temples of old has been completely overshadowed by a so-called scientific approach to development. Hence, the values by which modern society functions are those by which every little child must be educated.

Those who have difficulty in submitting to the concepts that are embodied in the well balanced and socially acceptable child, or young person, limit the ability of the Spirit to influence it's earthly form, this being the physical body. The Soul bridges the divide between personality and permanent consciousness, which is the Spirit of all beings, whether this is described as animal, vegetable, or mineral, or as a Man or Woman. The dictates of a materialistic world increase many fold the problems of acquiring the opportunity to handle the type of experience that actually is needed by a particular child.

Remember please that true growth is spiritual growth, not intellectual. Spiritual growth decides our progress on this plane of being. The Personality is only a chosen collection of genes, chosen in order to serve that life's proposed course.

I say chosen, to good purpose, believe me. Of this there is no question. Each and every one of you chose your parents, good or bad, as they may have been.

I think you will all agree that to make the utmost use of anything, we all try to make the optimum use of earlier knowledge in such a way as to both decide the best course of action, the best situation in which to take that action, and the best people with whom to interact in the process. In this way we reckon the chance of success is optimised. I am deliberately not saying guaranteed, because you need only consider the mercurial manner in which a chance happening in a particular scenario can take place. Life on Earth is never bound to respond unfailingly to our 'best laid plans'.

'As above, so below', from which contented people interpret that life on Earth is a manifestation of eternal life, and so it is. However, our 'best laid plans' do not always come to pass as we desire. Sometimes an influence beyond our control makes us alter course. For some this can be disastrous, and completely negates the purpose of that incarnation. For others a different set of becalming influences ensue, not always negative in effect, but resulting in a change of course and failure to achieve the port intended.

Like many an Earthly sailor, I found myself at times on foreign soil. I did not, however, lose the direction. So ultimately I dropped anchor in a friendly harbour, and fortunately stayed long enough to find my Grail.

Because some do not consciously seek to dabble in deep water, needless delay can occur. For others deep water holds no fear; the result is they dive in and flounder, or maybe drown if appropriate help is not aboard the mother craft. Have pity on these aspirants—they too are trying to become captains of life, and have temporarily been ship-wrecked. They must find another ship to sail. This means seeking another Earthly body to inhabit.

——— ★ ———

Part 1

**Living Through a Death Experience—
What is it Like?**

"I'm doing it my way!"

The first contact directly with Peter came on the evening of August 20th 1987, five months after he died. A small circle was held at Peter's home comprising Peter's parents, and two friends, one of whom was a trance medium. After a short while, Peter came to operate the medium's larynx, firstly at very low level, but later loud enough to be heard distinctly by the circle members, and to be recorded on tape. The voice slightly coloured by the medium's accent was completely that of Peter in intonation, and phrasing. Though a friend, the medium had never met Peter in life, nor heard his voice on a recording before.

Initial contact   20.8.87

"Hello. I'm doing it my way."

"Who are you please?"

"It's not quite like the old telephone. I've got a lot of love for my two ...ents (Parents). I'm sorry I've been so difficult at times. It's not what like I wanted, — it's so hard communicating, talking."

"Please confirm who you are."

"Pete, Peter the Fanatic."

"You are doing very well indeed."

"I've done a lot of learning. I thought I knew so much, and I didn't. I've really learnt. I've no wish to live again 'cos before I was born I'd chosen my life, and the best people to live it with."

"We loved having you Pete. Why did you have to go?"

"I haven't found out properly. I don't understand at all. Give me time. The way wasn't the chosen way. But, it just happened that way."

"Are you happy where you are?"

3

"Very happy. I cried a lot at the beginning. I knew how hard it was for you all."

"We didn't want to see you go."

"A lot of beautiful people are helping me do this. I'm not yet strong enough to be of much help."

"You will be. Please thank them all very much."

"I want to learn. I want to learn so much. I want to help others, and make sure they don't have to go this hard path."

"It was your chosen path. Have you met any members of our family?"

"I've met somebody, I'm not sure... I've met some helpers who helped to take the pain away."

"Please thank all who have helped, for us."

"I'll try and make my presence better known."

"Could you work telepathically, if I sit regularly."

"All I ask is that I have some time to learn. I don't want to get it wrong. I want to find out as much as I can. It is too easy to get wrong information and help. I've got to go soon. I can see all the energy, I'm using up too much. There is something I must tell you. I met a wonderful man. His name was Hugh. I've talked to him. I need time. I don't want to get it wrong. See, although my death was a shock, I sort of expected it. But, still I need time."

"Don't worry. Take your time."

"I enjoyed the funeral. Send Anne my love. It's been a very hard period of time. It all had meaning, it wasn't wasted, even some of the worst spells. Before I leave, ...love. You'll know it's me, you'll know, ... My love... I'll never... even though you'll not always hear my voice, I'll be there. God bless."

1. Post Accident

First impressions, Post accident, Leaving the Body, Pre-destined, Inquest, Destiny, Inevitability, Pre-cognition, Crossing the divide.

Peter describes his reaction to his accident, and subsequent death, and his passage into Summerland as a new arrival.

First impressions   7.9.89

"Love is an intense emotion, I had not understood so well until I knew I was leaving Earth. I could not believe my friends cared so much about my continuing to survive, and yet I left my body sensing an eminently more gracious environment than I had usually found on Earth.

I know this may sound ungracious in itself, but I must try to impress upon you the ecstasy that initially overwhelmed me. Nothing unpleasant was my lot. A feeling of love and freedom overwhelmed me. I had used my life to the full I felt, and was ready for this adventure.

I have described elsewhere the anguish that assailed me later. Just let that be for a moment, and come with me on a memorable journey into the beyond.

My heart goes out to those of you who see nothing but loss as you leave a departed loved one. Their experiences may not be the same as mine, but the love and the picture of beautiful surroundings will soon permeate all who have some good intentions in their heart.

I have given an impression of travelling through space. I tried to send back personal notes on what occurred. Please wait to criticise—Meditation could help you to experience reality too!

Some of my impressions are those of a new arrival. Some, like practical things on Earth, seem now to warrant a fresh process of analysis. The real world holds love in abundance, flowers in a profusion of indescribable colours. Vistas of unimaginable beauty, and limitless scope for learning and for giving.

Do not fear Death. Life here is as much what you make it, as it is on Earth. Here you will receive encouragement for your efforts, no matter how feeble or dynamic they may be. Total commitment to effort is the goal. The question of how far one can go, is only limited by oneself."

Post-accident   30.3.87

"Hullo Dad, I'm not very far away from you. Let's have a conversation. On the day I had my accident I had been into Hemel to get my Loudspeaker and parts. So I was very happy. I was thinking about this when I went through the lights. I just didn't remember them. The other car came across, and I didn't see it till too late. I knew I was going to hit it, and tried to ease back off the seat, but it was too late. Everything seemed against me.

Then I was out. When I woke up I could scarcely move. All my body hurt and my head seemed to have a great weight on it. Later I felt better. But, then I started to feel bad again. Just before I lifted out of my body I felt terrible."

"Directly after the accident you were unconscious. Can you remember anything of that period?"

"Yes, went towards a great, very strong light, leaving myself on the ground. A figure within the light spoke to me, and said,

'Do you want to remain here?'

I replied, 'No, I want to go back to see my family and friends.'

The figure said, 'You may go back for a short time. I will come again for you.' So, I returned to the body. And he came again with others and this time I went with them."

Leaving the body   22.8.87

"Hello Dad. We are together again."

"Tell me about your passing over, Pete. Did you experience the 'out of the body', and the 'dark tunnel' described by many people?"

"Not quite the same. I sort of came and stood by Mum and Fiona while they were rushing around with trolleys, and then I found myself lifted up by those wonderful people who had been with me for several days, and we drifted away over the hospital and Watford town.

6

Then I found myself touching down on what seemed to be hard earth again over here. No dark tunnel, no river Styx. Just gently floating with the others holding my arms through clouds, like when I used to do my flying! Yes, that's right Dad."

Pre-destined   23.8.87

"You said the other night in the circle that you did not yet know why you had to go when you did, but that it seemed to have been pre-destined. Perhaps, this will be clearer when you have moved through various stages, and are more in contact with your higher self."

"Yes I think probably so. Things are gradually becoming more clear, but there is so much to learn."

"Pete, your mother feels that you must have departed when she left the bedside, but she had no feeling that you were standing with her and Fiona."

"Well this all depends on your sensitivity, and maybe she was overwhelmed by her emotions. That's all for now... Pete."

The Inquest   9.9.87

"Dad, so at long last they have decided to hold the inquest! Well nothing new is likely to come from it. I shall be blamed for not stopping I suppose... 'driving without due care and attention', which I suppose is true as I was half asleep and not fully concentrating.

Lights have a hypnotic effect at night, and I think the colour of the car made it not show up until I was right on it. I should have stopped at the lights of course, and have only myself to blame for all the misery it has brought you two, Mum especially. I'm sorry, and for Anne too. Hope she gets on well with Mark. She deserves someone nice to look after her. I will always be around for her, but sometimes I don't seem able to reach her. Tell her to think of me more when she feels sad or worried, and I will come to her. And tell her to believe that we can communicate. That way it works better.

Love from Pete the fanatic!"

Destiny   11.9.87

"Dad, here I am again—Pete the fanatic! So the inquest came to the conclusion mine was accidental death. I think it was much more directed than that! They tell me here that very little is the result of chance. Most things are either the result of karma, or the result of a plan of living, or the person's free will. I think I would have died

7

about this time anyhow, from some cause if not the motorcycle. As you know I sort of had a feeling about this."

Inevitability   8.11.87

"Pete, you know about the inquest document that arrived?"

"Yes, I hope it didn't distress Mum and you too much. I do feel the responsibility of withdrawing from you, even though I had not expected it to go as it did. During the time I was unconscious at first I remember meeting a radiant person, like a light, who said, 'Go back', but I knew he only meant for a time. So don't blame the hospital staff too much. They couldn't have changed things. I realise that now. Please be happy for me, I hate sadness! Pete."

Pre-cognition   17.7.88

"Only know I arrived here feeling a question of my departure should have been discussed."

"By whom Pete?"

"Me!"

"You realised that you were going to depart from Earth, and we didn't? You felt on your side you should have indicated this? A bit of one thinks it would have been nice to know, but we may have been less relaxed."

"I think from all angles it was right that way, but I agreed before arriving here. I wanted to have time to say goodbye, but at the time I could not find the courage to tell you I knew."

"Did you have speech?"

"Yes."

"You started to speak a bit, and then you stopped. One wasn't sure it was a physical disability. Perhaps, it was best, we might not have coped."

"I prepared a speech for the occasion, but it seemed inappropriate."

"What were you going to say?"

"I wanted you to know I had planned the whole thing. I do not think you would have appreciated my motives at the time."

"No, Pete. It is hard enough to appreciate them now!"

"I want you to know I am always near when friends are visiting."

"It is still hard even now in spite of your close contact."

"I feel it will be easier for you because our communications are so good."

"They are indeed, probably better than when you were on Earth."

"I arrived here a month late. I should have departed just after Christmas, but plans went wrong. I intended to have an accident when I went climbing."

"Yes, there was a question of you going climbing after Christmas. You would have been a long way off. Was this a conscious change on your part?"

"Yes, I realised you would not get to the hospital in time to see me alive."

"We would have tried, but a climbing accident might have been a sudden death. We were 24 hours late in reaching you due to stomach upsets. You were sent up to London, and then back to Watford. We were later than we could have thought."

"I realised you were coming. It must have seemed a long time to you, but I was outside my body and could observe what you were doing."

"You were aware of what we were doing at home here?"

"Yes, got to go now."

Crossing the divide   18.7.88

"I am still intrigued, Pete as to whether or not you encountered this dark tunnel, or valley, at any stage in your departure to the other side. It has always seemed to me to be the means many people have of crossing the divide between Earth life, and Spirit life, though some accounts seem to miss it out."

"Well Dad, I certainly did not encounter a dark tunnel, or valley, during my death. When I came out of my body first of all, my encounter with the Being of Light was on or above the Earth level."

"You mean he came down to this level, Pete?"

"Yes, and the second time was when they came down to the hospital while I was in bed, and stood around me. I knew it wasn't long then. When it finally happened, and I was sick, they lifted me so gently out of my body, and we just rose through the hospital which sort of opened up, and went on till we touched down here.

I had stayed long enough with Mum to watch them trying to start my heart, before we finally left for home here—no dark tunnel, or darkness of any sort—all light and brightness!

I think the image of darkness is for those who haven't got much idea about life and death, which, I am sorry to say, means most people in Western countries. Death to them is sort of awful, a dark oblivion, so perhaps the valley of the shadow of death is a sort of symbol to them, and their passage through it dependent on having some spark of the Christ Power to keep them going. There are some that don't make it and are lost in the darkness. We have to rescue them, and this is the work that is suggested for the group, if you come together again, as I have a feeling you will."

Summary

The environment Peter found on leaving his body was beautiful, gracious, and full of love. Death is far from oblivion; life after death is what one makes it.

2. Life in Summerland

Conditions in Summerland, Weather, Ease of living, Changing surroundings, Travel by thought, Power of thought, Learning opportunities, Loving attitude, Time to rest time to learn, A Home of your own, Sacred Geometry, Marriage and children, Divine birth, Christmas, Religion - Angels and the Christ Spirit, 'Love one another', Passage of Time and events, Rapid reading, Higher and lower planes, Spiritual realms, Art, 'Photographic' images, Sport and competition, Rescue work, Psychic dabbling.

The wonder of the life experienced in Summerland as it first appeared to Peter are described, and summarised at the end of the chapter. Summerland is the name given to the realm experienced after the physical body is released at death.

Conditions In Summerland

"I am now about to describe the paradise you all call 'Heaven'. Please try to set aside all conscious ideas of your arrival at the gates of a Heaven full of Cherubs, Angels, a group of Seraphims, and a fatherly figure presiding over the company. I want to indicate, to convey, the feeling of wonder which fills one's being on finding oneself surrounded by a host of unknown, but completely relaxed faces; unless one can sense youth's carefree beginnings, there is no way to describe the sensation. Friends and relatives may not appear. A conscious evangelical approach, salvation by faith alone, has possibly never been your way of thinking. How are you to comprehend the love apparently surrounding you when you may find yourself dependent on such strangers?

It can, I forewarn you, actually alarm you. After all, a worm can turn, a serpent bite and kill. Was not one found in the 'Garden of Eden'? How very suspicious you can become of smooth talking, courteous people of only limited credentials? I must ask you to abstain from seeking the 'arm of the Law'—truth to tell, the Men in Blue do not exist here. My friends are patient, they have a sense of

11

humour. They will smile, and promise you some family contact when you are ready."

The Weather

Differences in the weather conditions from those on Earth:~

"With us Dad, there are no seasons as such. I thought it strange at first, but one soon gets used to it. There is steady growth throughout the year. It seems to be self-regulated by the plant family concerned. When the plant reaches its zenith, it just fades away and is replaced by a new plant growing up. There are differences from day to day, but never dying leaves. It is the species which matters—the plant group rather than an individual plant.

As you know it is always fine and sunny over here, like a fresh summer day, in comparison to your variable climate.

Well, I have discovered that it is possible to go to an area where it is raining at times, and sunny at other times, quite variable. Also, other areas where snow falls at times. These areas are inhabited by people who long for changes in the weather. They tend to be for early arrivals back here who miss the climatic changes on Earth. In general, most things from Earth are available here until people grow out of wanting them."

Ease of living   11.5.87

The lack of difficulties experienced on Earth:~

"Yes, I have changed a little, matured more I think, and find myself drawing on earlier lives, and using experiences, talents perhaps, from some of these lives, which I had forgotten about when I was on Earth with you.

Things here are rather like they are on Earth, but much easier, and I have to guard against being lazy—stretched out in the radiant light—delightful!"

"Do you get any such germs or viruses where you are?"

"No, anything like that apparently collects in the dark lands, the 'Winterlands'[1] as Paul Beard calls them. That is another blessing of this area. You can have no conception how easy life can be here. The problem is finding difficulties and challenges to surmount. This is why so many here do their best to help those on Earth, or just

---

1   From *Living On* by Paul Beard, Bantam Books.

passing over. This is one of the few areas—together with work in the Winterlands—where challenges do exist."

Changing surroundings   22.8.87

Surroundings are similar to those on Earth, but are changed by thought:~

"What do your surroundings seem to be like, Pete?"

"Much the same as on Earth, but more changeable, just by thinking about them."

"Did you find difficulty in getting used to them?"

"No. Much nicer feeling about them than about most places on Earth."

"How did you find things when you first arrived on the other side?"

"Well Dad, I had expected a world rather like the Earth zone, and this is the case. But it all seemed rather dreamy at first, like when you first wake up on Earth. But then it sharpened up later. Somehow I think it's all a bit unreal, and will change."

"How is your memory for Earthly things, Peter?"

"Well, it certainly tends to fade a bit at times. Not so much for people that I knew well, or major things that happened, but details which were not very important to me. It is sometimes beginning to seem like a dream I had, though, of course, we don't dream here like I did on Earth. If we rest or sleep it is just a period of release of consciousness. Though some things seem the same here, the life is really not the same at all."

"Have you met people from higher areas, Peter?"

"Apart from Hugh[1], you mean? Well, occasionally a being who is obviously, from their brightness of their aura, from a more advanced area, does visit us. There is a most wonderful feeling of love and compassion that goes with them. Rather like some of the Steiner teachers, though much more accentuated."

24.3.88

"How nearly like our Earth world is the world you live in Peter?"

"So nearly alike that many people have the greatest difficulty in knowing they have died: Streets, houses, fields, scenery, all alike. Though the absence of cars must make the first difference they notice, I suppose. I'm used to the calm peace and love that pervades

1   See *Appendix of Names.*

this world, but for someone catapulted here from your Earth it must seem the greatest change, I think."

2.8.88

"Is the world around you still similar to this world on Earth, or has it changed to any extent?"

"While acknowledging that it is basically an illusion, the world I live in is much the same as that on Earth, at least on the surface. There are fundamental differences (such as this ability to alter things by thought), but in general it appears at a first glance to be the same.

I could at this stage inhabit a different world, and I sometimes feel this urge to move to more spiritual planes, but until you and Mum come over here, I shall stay at this level. There is Anne to consider too, and even when we three are together again, I would wish to stay in close contact with Anne, while she wants me.

Now, one could do this from a different plane, but it is more convenient from this world. I also need to fulfil my promise to help mankind conquer the fear of death. Hopefully, this will be the result of this book and of talks that you and Mum will give in the future."

Travel by thought 22.12.87

Thinking about a place will get you there:~

"What do you think of the idea that seems to be prevalent, that your surroundings, where you are, are individual to the spirit inhabiting them?"

"Well, to some extent I suppose that's true, but since the surroundings here, at any rate, are shared with other people; for example I share this bit of world with others, though they go off at times somewhere I can't follow; since there is this sharing locally, the surroundings can't be individual, can they?

The transport system is quite wonderful though, 'cos I only have to think of going somewhere, and hold that thought steady, and I find myself transported there.

There are limits, the area must be much the same spiritual level as I am now, neither too high nor too low, though it's easier to go low than too high; high and low in the sense of spiritual levels, including expansion of consciousness.

When I come to you as I am doing now, only a part of me is transported down, and there seems to be a sort of *ray of love* between us, down which I slide, am attracted.

14

Most of me remains in this world. In a sense we are always connected. You have only to think of me, and I get the feeling, which is nice.

So, think of me and send love many times a day, and the channel between us will be kept open."

14.8.88

"Over here physical effort is not needed. One visualises what is required, and it just sort of happens."

"Don't you miss the physical effort then Peter?"

"Not really. It all seems rather strange at first, but one soon gets used to it. And remember, our body is not of the same physical material as on Earth, so lack of exercise is not a problem.

I suppose on Earth someone from, say, the past centuries would find riding round in a car strange at first, so here the use of visualisation to transport oneself can seem strange."

"In occult literature, it is stated one cannot go to any place one hasn't been before. Does this mean in an Earth life?"

"Most people will not venture unless something is familiar."

" Is this a question of having confidence in travel?"

"Yes, or if one has been in an Earth life, things are familiar."

"A recent Earth life or one long ago?"

"Yes if one has been escorted on this side, then you know what appears to be familiar. Otherwise a definite risk of confusion exists. So one isn't totally free to go where one wants!"

The Power of Thought — a summary   10.9.89

Thought is the key to immediate transportation, and communication. Thoughts can have a beneficial or destructive effect:~

"I presume you all go on holiday at times. The preparations are considerable. The luggage weighs a great deal, and its contents assume complete pride of place in the consciousness of the particular people involved. After all, a big part of the holiday is to see, and be seen. Embarrassment ensues if one is inadequately prepared, and arriving unprepared for an activity can be fraught with danger if we are minus the appropriate tools for the job.

Now for us, none of these headaches arise. I will try to explain in basic terms. You are usually focussed on the pleasure of the journey, though some might be preoccupied with working out an itinerary. For us work is synonymous with feeling contented, or happy, as you term it. To do our work, or to achieve certain understanding, we need to join with others of like intention, or with Earth folk who need our guidance. I feel I should not say 'need'. Earth folk seldom feel the need, but we sense places in which we might give out some supporting vibrations to advantage.

Our vision soaks up the complexities of Earth life, and our specific interests focus our vision—hence a pull to action is usually felt. Of course there is no need to cart our 'luggage' around and stay for a month of discussion. Our decision to help is spontaneous, and with it comes our relevant vibration.

Thoughts have a power of their own. This applies to your thoughts too. Though you may be reluctant to take this too literally, I assure you, *kind thoughts heal, and malicious thoughts destroy.*

Our thoughts immediately bring us into close contact with the perpetrator. Hence, to sense the call, is to arrive. To feel the need, is to answer one's beleaguered companion with an attempt to help.

Do not think relatives are saturated with their departed family because they have problems. *The love and acceptance of need must be linked.*

In the long run, thought is the key to immediate transportation. It can even happen on Earth!"

Learning opportunities   12.10.87

There are endless opportunities for learning and applying one's learning, for the good of others and to the advancement of oneself:~

"Really, there is so much to learn about over here! No end to it. Apart from communications, I'm also learning about ancient history, going back through the civilizations that have come and gone. The joy of it is that one can go back and live the life that those people led, and really appreciate their problems.

I go to classes on history, and the way this affects present day Man: relationships between nations and peoples; the way one should relate to others and live one's lives; the true structure of Man and of the Earth and the Universe. Also, on the true science of existence, not the limited sort taught on Earth."

"How do you see your future now, Pete?"

"It seems that the best thing to do is to learn, and then apply that learning to help people. The other way is to try and use one's knowledge to influence the way the world goes, to try and stop all this emphasis on material possessions, and help people think more of one another."

"Peter, can you tell how many of the Souls around you are working like you to advance their abilities?"

"Well, I have met a lot of people who are obviously out to have a good time here. As I told you some time back it is only too easy to put one's feet up and rest in the sun, or enjoy oneself in other ways. On the other hand the classes I go to are well attended, though I suppose by a relatively small number.

It is nice to rest in peace here, but I don't think I could do so for too long. There is a sort of urgency in the air at the colleges to learn and advance.

But, advancement comes from putting into practise what one learns. This is a must, otherwise learning alone can drag you down, not up. If you know something which can benefit others, and you fail to apply it when you could or should, there is a risk of incurring negative karma. *Knowledge is released on the understanding that it will be applied to the benefit of mankind, discarnate, or incarnate.* Anyway, I feel I want to know as much as I can, and apply it!

As I told you, I was amazed when I came here how little people on Earth know of the truth, and how much of their apparent knowledge is illusion. The picture of the Earth and Universe is totally inadequate, and only one aspect of the reality that is apparent here. You all have an awful lot to learn when you arrive back here."

A loving attitude   17.2.88

Keeping a loving attitude can dispel the solidity of Earthly things:~

"How does your world really appear to you?"

"After being here a short time one notices the differences from Earth. The light around is different. People appear differently, each one has his or her own light. They seem to appear or disappear at the drop of a hat. The whole feeling and atmosphere is clean, fresh, and loving.

As I said before the emphasis is on love between people. On Earth one felt stress and antipathy between people, in many situations, much less so in the Steiner schools. Here, one is surrounded on all sides by love and caring.

But yes, initially after dying, one might well be back on the Earth again, and as you know from what you have read, many people just cannot believe they are dead. Eventually, they have to admit things are different. But, the first impressions are of the solidity of Earthly things. I suppose it must be that they slowly expand their consciousness and realise this is not Earth.

Talking to people who do rescue work from this side, this aspect is one they often have to help to dispel. While people still think they are on Earth they continue to act in Earthly ways. Only when they realise they have crossed the divide, can they begin to progress towards the light.

I would urge you to move as far in our direction as possible before you come here. Read, and read, Bailey and Steiner particularly.[1] Meditate, and do as much good for others as possible. It is vitally important here—all other material things just do not matter.

Your attitude to the Spiritual is all important, so please keep cheerful, it will help others in the world who have not the access to a channel like this."

A time to rest, time to learn   9.3.88

"A number of other folk have communicated, and certainly most did not seem to be doing much with their lives now, whereas you seem to be very active."

"Well, I find the opportunities over here to be endless Dad, and as you well know it is not in my nature to stay still for long.

It is really all so interesting and wonderful here as well as being more beautiful than you can imagine. Also, I feel a sort of urge within me to get on, learn more, and advance further, *see* further if you like.

But, I can quite understand why many others do not want to be bothered. They may have had a hard or difficult life on Earth, and there is no pressing reason why they should do anything more here. They don't need to eat, to sleep, or even to bother about a house. The weather is always fine, continually, so there is no need of shelter. So their life often consists of drifting round, revelling in the beauty, meeting other people, all of whom are friendly, to a greater or lesser degree, and just being!

After a while they may change and think about advancement, and that can bring thoughts of a return to Earth to improve various characteristics—hard to contemplate—but for now it is the 'Good Life'.

I did this for a short while, but began to get almost satiated or 'bored', dare one say it?. So, as you know, I started to go to lectures

1   See *Recommnended Reading* for Alice A. Bailey and Rudolph Steiner.

which immediately expanded my interests, showed me how little I know, and helped to satisfy my search for knowledge.

Don't worry! The others will all come to this, but in their own good time. For the 'now' they need to enjoy drifting and roaming. Love Peter."

A Home of your own   End '87

Peter describes the domestic surroundings and housing arrangements one might encounter:~

"What are your surroundings like to you at the moment?"

"Well, I'm sitting comfortably on a sofa, not unlike the one you have at home, and reclining, so that I can bring you to mind and communicate. I'm in Mary's[1] house, as she has kindly offered to house me for the moment. The room is a big squarish one, with a high ceiling, like the house at Herne Bay. The view from the windows is superb, green fields stretching away towards the distant mountain ranges.

This house is on the edge of what you might call a town, suburbs, only these are very beautiful. There are other people living quite close, and we often meet and talk.

There are no cars or motorcycles around. They are not necessary for transport.

I haven't been in too much of a hurry for my own house, as I am quite happy where I am, sharing Mary's house. Also, the sort of house one can live in depends on your personality from the last life. There are teams of people over here, who will build your house, but it must be suitable for you. I think mine will be of the sort of shape of the Georgian period, large rooms, high and nicely proportioned. Outside, not too big, but again nicely proportioned, the Golden Rule (*see 'Sacred Geometry'*).

I don't mind if it's in a terrace, with neighbours each side. But, as I say, I am not in a hurry and perhaps it may change a little before completion. The main thing is that it's got to be me, or I can't live in it!

I like sharing a house at present and at times I need someone to give me confidence, because things are different here. At other times it is all so interesting, and exciting I'm well away. I expect as I get used to life here, and sort of mature, I will like living in my own place.

1   See *Appendix of Names.*

Although this seems like home I have been told that it is really all illusion, and will eventually change, or may be I will change and not need it. Anyway, I am quite happy here at present."

Sacred Geometry in architecture 16.2.88

"Have you had an opportunity to study subjects like Sacred Geometry, Peter?"

"Only a little so far. Of course, I knew a certain amount about Sacred Geometry from the Steiner schools, but have not gone much more deeply into it. It is obviously part and parcel of all the buildings here, and they glow with the energy built into them by virtue of their geometry.

I suppose this is more obvious here, and probably because whatever Earthly builders did they could only get the geometry roughly right with the coarse materials used. Whereas, here the geometry and measurements are exact, and thus the energy flows in from the cosmos.

Over here, building is still to the classical principles of the 'Golden Rule'. It has to be in accordance with Sacred Geometry for power to flow into it. A building without such power-flow is cold and unattractive to us."

Marriage and children 22.7.88

Marriage in Heaven is a linking of Souls at a high mental level. Children, and the part they play:~

"Do you have marriages in Heaven? If so, do you produce children?"

"We do not have marriages in the sense that you have on Earth, a church service, or civil ceremony. There are no 'physical' sexual relationships. What we do have is a linking together of Souls at a high mental level, where this is the choice of the people concerned.

There is mental and emotional union, which is much stronger, and longer lasting than mere physical sex, and a sort of marriage ceremony, invoking the blessing of God, through certain of the higher brethren. This union may last for as long as it is deemed to be in the best spiritual interests of the Souls concerned, and does not hinder their individual progress.

As regards children, the creation of new Spirits and Souls is the prerogative of God, but their education is something many people delight to do."

"Don't they, the children, miss the warmth and protection of a family life?"

"No, because they are surrounded by Souls anxious to give them love and affection, and guide them gently in the right way to grow. They join in groups with other children, and learn together. Eventually they incarnate, and begin the cycle that we all follow.

If a child dies soon after being born, he or she, is welcomed back into the group it left, with great joy. As many children on Earth have traumatic experiences, they often have to be helped to assimilate these experiences by Souls appointed to this delicate task.

There is a necessity for all of us to experience the bad as well as the good in human nature. This has been so throughout the ages, and is not just a feature of modern life. It is just more prominent in the news nowadays than it ever was. Our tears are for those children being born into the world, not for those leaving it!"

Children and divine birth   9.2.90

"A lot of confusion is in assessment of the term 'child'. I must attempt to explain the concept. I do not mean in Earthly terms, that is obvious. But, when you speak of children, you are meaning people young in Earth years. A lot of difference exists between that and the true situation.

Because, if one has lived many times before, one cannot be experiencing most things for the first time. Only death has temporarily expunged things that were familiar, and has substituted less arduous experiences. To every individual who can itemise the pangs of growing up, it does not give any huge problem. I would suggest that for a total beginner, things could be more difficult. So, I want to differentiate between just *starting out*, and *re-starting* an Earth life.

For reasons that one cannot give in terms that can be understood totally, fresh beings are occasionally needed to undertake tasks of considerable importance, but for which a question of 'vision' is needed. Highly developed people are not always readily able to resume life on Earth again, for reasons that are outside the scope of this book. In such rare circumstances, 'marriage' here can create the environment in which such a spark of God's divinity can develop to a point at which incarnation does not require the aeons of time to master the intricacies of true humility and service to Humanity.

I refer to the 'Divine purpose' only to answer a question on Heavenly marriage.

Children who are deprived of development on Earth for whatever reason, know very quickly on returning here, that the demands of spiritual growth require them to learn rapidly to develop beyond the point of their departure. Much love and guidance is provided here.

So, although to those who knew them on Earth, they would continue to reappear as originally known, they are gradually reclaiming all that has gone before, and will ultimately be seen by us as an energy that is greater and more precious in relationship to God."

Christmas in Summerland   25.12.87

"I understand that Christmas is totally a spiritual occasion over here, in the sense that it celebrates the spirits of the Earth, Nature, plants and animals. Also, the *Christ Spirit*—but not the birth of Christ—'cos that occurred later in the year.

One tries to do something special for someone else. Something within one's own power which they find difficult to accomplish. That's difficult when they are more advanced than you are. But anyway they appreciate the thought and effort. It's a time of rejoicing and renewal through the Christ Power at the Winter Solstice."

Religion - Angels and the Christ Spirit   17.1.88

"Morning Dad!"

"Peter, how much do you come in contact with the religious elements? For instance you haven't mentioned being surrounded by angels playing their harps! Or, even contact with higher divinity such as Christ?"

"No Dad, a lot of the traditional picture people on Earth have of Heaven is surmise built up by the churches over the centuries. Angels, or Devas certainly exist, and can be contacted here more easily than on Earth, but they are rather different to us, being *points of power dedicated to a certain purpose.*

There are harps here, but mainly in orchestras, which one can go to hear if so inclined. Some lone harpists, who play for the pleasure of others.

The Christ power certainly exists as a wonderful stream of energetic light in which one can be totally refreshed, *pure love.* But, one is scarcely more near to the source here than on Earth. One has to move a long way up the planes to approach it more closely.

However, as I have said in the past, everyone is so nice to everyone else here—so much love for others—that it is like being in Heaven.

Hugh and Mary tell me that there are so many higher planes of consciousness beyond this one, in which one becomes 'refined' in spirit. It is all rather breathtaking! We have no doubt that God—the greatest source—exists, but we realise more and more how far we have to travel and change to approach the Divine planes."

'Love one another'   7.2.88

"How much do you come in contact with what is known as religion on Earth, Pete? Do you have religious services?"

"Well, those who belong to orthodox religious groups continue to hold services as they did on Earth, so I am told. We just give our own private thanks to God for the wonderful world we are in—many times over—and try to maintain *natural law,* and love for others.

There is some wonderful church type music here Dad. I'm sure you will delight in it when you arrive back here. There are churches here which some people like to go to, those from a church going group on Earth. But, we think of God as the ultimate power, without any religious ceremonies, and the Christ Power, a wonderful loving light, is available to everyone here. Christ's message 'to love one another' *is* put into practise here."

The passage of Time and event   2.1.88

The passage of time is subjective. It is marked by the link between one event and another and our own free will to choose our path:~

"Seems strange writing '88 in place of '87. I suppose it is only twelve years till we have to write '00, or 2000!"

"Well it doesn't make much difference to us Dad, as I said before. I think the passage of time is marked by the change in people as much as by events. That's not very well put. What I mean is that people develop and expand their awareness, or most people here do. Then they are able to move around more easily, that is into higher regions; higher in the sense of spirituality, not position. Before this expansion they are limited to the region they feel comfortable in.

So, when I first arrived I stayed on the one level, and did not wander far. Now, I feel I can move up at least a little if I want to, without feeling uncomfortable. It's a sort of different dimension of awareness that I think either did not exist on Earth, or was much less obvious. So, that improvement in 'mobility' marks the passage of time since I arrived, as much as the events that I have experienced here. I don't follow day by day on your plane except in so far as you contact me. That's why it is best if you make this regular contact. Does that explanation seem to make sense, Dad?"

"Yes Pete. I think you are right. This sort of change does take place here on Earth, but is much less obvious, and would not be thought of as a 'dimension'. But, as you are what we call 'thought', I can see it has much greater significance for you."

1.6.88

"Good morning Peter! What do you want to discuss this morning?"

"Time! For you on Earth it is divided up into regular packets of night and day, weeks, months, and seasons. Each is fairly clear cut, though I remember times when summers seemed like winter. Here there are no such divisions, but we are aware, if we think about it, of your division, whether it is day or night with you."

"Didn't it seem strange to you Peter, when you first arrived? You used to make full use of your sleep at home, from the early morning onwards!"

"Well, yes, I suppose so. But, I soon got used to the idea of just carrying on."

"Don't you feel tired at times, and don't you wish to be on your own at times?"

"Yes, but one can shut one's eyes and rest, on the occasions one feels like it. As for being on one's own, there is a state one can enter which indicates to others that one does not wish to be disturbed. Everyone respects this except God, who is welcome anyway!"

"For us on Earth, you remember the passing of time is of great importance, and interest. People's lives are totally governed by time, the aging process is intimately tied up with its passage. How is it with you?"

"This is one of the great blessings of being here. The only occasions on which we have to worry about time is when we contact you. In fact, our morning and evening meetings govern me more than anything else."

"Oh! I'll try harder not to be late, Pete! How then do you know our Earth time?"

"That comes as a sort of feeling. We could of course come to your level and look at Big Ben, but that's not necessary. We just think, and a voice says:

'The time sponsored by Accurist is now...'"

24

"Isn't it boring just going on and on into eternity Pete?"

"We don't find it so. One can always look back at past events here, and see them as present events, or even at future events. If we think hard we can even see and feel them in reverse order—that is cause following event—they all exist. It is us that can choose to experience the action in any way we wish, and draw from that experience what we need."

"You say all events exist. What about free will then to choose?"

"Yes, we all have that by endowment from God. All events exist, and so do all possible events. One can weave a given path through life, or one can choose to vary that path. The choice is ours. We can activate the possible events into actual experiences according to how we choose our path."

2.6.88

"As you know we co-exist with the physical world."

"So, do you go round with the Earth's rotation? And if you go round with the Earth, why doesn't the Sun's light get stronger and weaker as you rotate, giving night and day?"

"Well, I'm not an expert on 'Spiritual Geophysics', but it seems that our light does not come direct from the Sun in the form of radiation that yours on Earth does, but comes from a light source *charged up* by the Sun, like a battery, and releasing light continually. That is why here one never gets blinded by the Sun, but the light is pleasantly diffused. In consequence, we still have light here when you on Earth are in darkness.

We certainly don't rush past you at high speed, except in our thoughts, and then generally through time. Though we can travel the Earth at high speed if we so wish, as we travel the Summerland. Anyway, that's what I understand at present; may be subject to amendment as I learn more."

16.7.88

"As I think I told you some while back (I was going to say time) the passage of time here is not evenly marked as it is on Earth by the apparent movement of the Sun. The passage of time is much more subjective.

So on Earth it has an effect on human consciousness generally unrecognised. It is only because we keep looking at the clock that we know with any certainty that, say, one hour has elapsed on Earth. That hour can go, apparently, very quickly (too quickly for convenience sometimes), or, apparently, very slowly (too slowly) at other times. This is because, subjectively, we try to get an objective measure of time by thinking of the activity we have undergone.

We are also limited by the movement of the Sun, the Earth's rotation. So it may be a very short, or very long, day, week month, or year.

In an accident situation time can seem to stretch out as our activity to avoid that accident is frenetic. In other words, our conscious measure of time on Earth is very subjective.

Oh yes, our body's biological clock is another measure of time we have on Earth. Not so here. We have no body—*no physical body*—a totally different biological constitution. And we don't go in for clocks and clock-watching!

Events happen here, usually in the same sequence as on Earth, (much more easily than on Earth) but also in reverse sequence!

Our life is a subjective one, so time can easily stretch out, or contract, compared to Earth. So, it is often difficult to know what the passage of time on Earth has been. We rely on you on Earth to *send us the feeling* that it is now time for something, say a meeting.

Dad, you used to talk about the timelessness of life on the West coast of Scotland, as it used to be. If you can imagine that sort of life, only much more so, that gives some idea of the bliss of being here. I used to experience it to a certain degree on my camping holidays. Now I enjoy it at all times!"

Rapid reading   2.3.88

How one can absorb knowledge by rapid reading:~

"Hallo Peter! How do you get on with reading now?"

"Well, there is a wonderful library here with copies of all the books ever published, so one can delve into anything. I seem to be able to assimilate the knowledge contained in a book almost by intuition, *just by holding the book and tuning in.* Perhaps, it's 'rapid reading', or like a talking book."

"You may remember one has to work rather harder at reading on Earth, and then only part of the substance of the book stays in one's mind."

"You are wrong Dad! All that you read or do on Earth remains with you, it is the *recall mechanism* which often seems to get stuck, or be rather slow to work. Over here, because there is no material brain through which we can block recall, no sooner do we decide on what we want to remember, than it comes flooding back. The flood can be instantly controlled as well so we don't get overwhelmed.

This is the advantage of an inertia-free subtle body: exact placing and recall of memory."

Higher and lower planes   14.2.88

What lies beyond the life Peter leads at present:~

"I have in mind Dad, that you would be interested in what lies beyond the sort of life I am living now.

Well, in the one direction, that of restricted consciousness, and the lack of the driving power of love, lies a barren gloomy, dark area, which I approached once with a guide. We didn't go far into it, because it made me feel ill, and Mary, very wisely decided I was not strong enough at that time to stand it. People lived there who had not moved far enough into the light to come into our area, I was told.

In the other direction, that of expanded consciousness, is an area of brilliant light, and much greater spirituality. Again, the guide took me towards this area, but I found my strength insufficient to stand the light and power coming from this area for more than a few minutes.

It is inhabited by beings much more advanced than myself. As I understand things this is the area we will all eventually move into; the sixth form! So, that is what I am working towards."

"Do you have germs and illnesses in the Summerland Peter, or are these something you leave behind on death?"

"Very much the latter Dad. We are all quite healthy here, though in the areas that are called the Winterlands, that I mentioned to you as being barren and cold, illness and germs do exist. Still rather different to your Earth illnesses, because of no physical body. A sort of disturbance of our body which makes one feel bad.

It is a result of wrong thinking by the souls residing there. I suppose similar to the wrong use of, and wrong action to, one's physical body on Earth. Anyway, all of us here are healthy and happy, – Peter."

Spiritual realms   27.5.88

"What's the subject today?"

"Progress, spiritual progress. I have been having a brief preview of some of the higher spheres, in company with a guide, just to show me where we are heading; quite indescribable in Earthly terms.

The brilliance of light, to my sight, was quite... almost dazzling, and yet not so. Absolutely radiant beings, and the feeling of love, was overwhelming. I felt quite faint, although we were there for only a very short time. One will have to condition oneself by stages before being even a novice in those spheres.

This is where my project with you will come in, if we complete it successfully, which we will. In the meantime I remain at this level, to learn and work."

"What else do you do Peter?"

"I travel round to see places and people on Earth, or in other parts of our world."

"On your own?"

"Quite often, or in company with a guide."

"Do you ever get into difficulties?"

"Occasionally, one finds enclaves of people who are not happy in their lives, and the atmosphere can affect one, particularly if one tries to help them. However, there is a 'rescue service' that one can call on in emergencies to help one return."

Art   10.2.88

Whether artistic abilities can be improved in Summerland:~

"What about artistic standards in your area, Peter? Is it possible for someone to vastly improve their ability to play a musical instrument for instance, or to paint, or write to much higher standards? Or, is this something one has to return to Earth life to do?"

"As far as I can make out Dad, one can work to improve artistic abilities at any form of art, here, just as well as on Earth. Probably better, but it does depend what your spirit decides is the most important thing for you to do next while you are here."

'Photographic' images   10.2.88

No need for Photography, wishing will produce an excellent picture:~

"Morning Dad!"

"One thing I have been meaning to ask, Peter, is do you have 'cameras' and 'photography' in your present area?"

"No Dad, we have no need of cameras. If one wants to see someone, or somewhere, as it was at a given time, just the *wishing to do so* will bring the vision to mind.

For instance, if one wanted to see someone at different periods, these visions will appear like a cine shot, and one can then hold any particular one as long as one likes. So, the system is really like a very sophisticated video film—no, really a very sophisticated video, or camera is a poor imitation of our ability over here!"

Sport and competition   22.8.88

There is no 'competition' in Summerland:~

"We were rather surprised that you do not have organised games like cricket or football, or even athletics like running!"

"Well, if you think about it Dad, they are all 'cults' of the physical body, and having no physical body to deal with, there is no need of such physical exercises. Also, a lot of them involve competition, and there is no competition here, nor was there in the Steiner schools. Each soul is taken on his or her merits as an individual without comparison to others.

What is worse is that so many 'Sports' these days also involve large sums of money as a reward for winning, and as you know 'money' has no value here. Also, some sports involve masses of spectators, who, driven on by the unbridled emotions, released by the success or otherwise of their favourite teams, end up by slaughtering each other. That wouldn't go down well here in a land of caring and loving; might be reserved for 'Hell' though!"

Rescue work   3.11.88

Rescue work is a fulfilling way of helping beings in trouble. It can occur suddenly and sporadically:~

"Who have you been rescuing, Pete, recently? Can you tell us anything about it?"

"The first one was an old man who had got stuck at the Earth level having died of heart failure following too much whiskey. He had never believed in heaven, or hell, in fact he dismissed the whole notion. So when he found himself out of his body, he couldn't understand it at all. Nor could he understand why the attempt to drink more whiskey was a failure. It so depressed him that he had no chance of rising to our level, but sat there on his bed moping! I had to approach him very carefully and tactfully, as he was rather irascible, and not very high in level at all. My own experience in drinking whiskey was helpful, and I was able to persuade him to go with me. With help we got him over to our side. He is now in a rest home for alcoholics recovering well.

There have been several others as well. Tell you about them another time."

Psychic dabbling and rescue work   9.11.88

"I had to depart at short notice last night to a rescue job."

"Are you going to say anything about this?"

"Yes, an old woman...

"How old Pete?"

"Oh, about sixty... had been dabbling in magic and got herself into a condition where she was possessed by a rather low entity. A priest had been called in to release the entity, exorcise it, but was unsuccessful. He wasn't so spiritual himself!

A plea was put up for help, so several of us formed a rescue party. After quite a struggle the entity was persuaded to let go, and went off to the area it was meant to be in. The woman was given help on the inner levels to cleanse her system of the magic energies which had dragged her down. She is still alive and recovering. We hope this will have been a lesson she learns.

You know these magic energies can be very powerful, and can wreck a human being's etheric system. You are best to stay well clear of them."

Summary

Peter's summarises his view on the process of his dying and how he reconciled it with his purpose and desire to help others to cope with death and accept the actuality of a continued existence. He also suggests ways to help make the most of life in thanksgiving:~

"I had an idea that some form of life actually existed, other than on Earth. I could not recall any details. I appear to have tried to explain queer experiences I had on Earth by attempting to link special events with some form of 'overseer'.

I decided I would be quite interested in exploring death. Life seemed to be full of problems once one became an adult, and so many of them seemed to me to be of little real consequence.

You are going to possibly resent that comment on civilization, but I must tell you that in my sleeping hours, I felt I had a life elsewhere, and daily pressing demands for intellectual pursuits seemed irrelevant to the tragic experiences that actually gripped many people in the world.

I feel now that my contact at night time was made here where I now have yesterday's memories available if I want to tap into them. Strange that one can have some awareness like this, and some underlying experiences, and yet find this world has little that is initially familiar when one actually arrives back again, for that is what happens.

I have already said I almost panicked on finding myself unable to communicate totally freely with those with whom I had been close. Somehow, although I had no recollection of a life after death, I also seem to have thought that I could keep in touch with Earth. To explain this is not possible in a logical way. I suppose that in one's spirit body, one feels so little changed, that a knowledge of one's presence seems most obvious, and to find oneself alive and desperate to give out happiness, as opposed to despair, and be quite unable to convey this to those closest to you, is initially a horrific experience.

For some, a period of support and care is needed. I refer to those who absorbed little in Earth life that could prepare them for the actual possibility of a continued existence; also, those affected by long illness.

31

I found myself fit and well, decidedly more aware of intense love than I had ever experienced on Earth at the hands of strangers, yet full of remorse on account of others' distress. This caused me many tears and much self-recrimination. I was listened to, and told that I would find I could help to ease the broken hearts, and at the same time make some contribution to life on Earth. This is the purpose of my attempt to provide a scenario of my consciousness, not only for the benefit of those who are just about to follow me, but also to widen the field of vision of those who construct Humanity's future on Earth by virtue of their policies."

The way is long

"The path combines lots of effort with lots of adventure. It has pitfalls in plenty. Both snakes and devils abound, but they are of your own making!

Beware of complacency. It will get you a comfortable seat on a stationary train. An enquiring approach may well display serpents under many windows. But they are to be faced, and always your own efforts can enable you to join a train that moves, and from which the vistas continually unfold revealing wondrous beauty, and truths not accessible to those still sitting in the comfort of the stationary train.

On many occasions, as one gazes out of a window, not always from a train, one is occupied with a burden associated with daily life. True vision is blurred, possibly extinguished totally. Such aggravation limits the extent to which one's higher self can function.

To the generous platitudes given out by an idle spirit, such as, 'Gosh, the Sun is shining!', or 'Oh dear, another wet day!', I will attempt to add one slightly less ignominious:

Like many folk on Earth, I too used to do just that. May I suggest an alternative approach? As you acknowledge the existence of a world outside your own precious domain, lift up your eyes. Take a moment to pause. If you feel so inspired, sing 'Alleluia!' The sound will send loving vibrations through the universe.

From deference to you being too embarrassed to react in such a way, I suggest instead that in your heart you give thanks to God for his bounteous gifts. Like so many, totally unconscious, much that is freely available to you remains untapped during your day. An appreciation of this should in itself bring a smile to your lips. Go for it, and your effort will not go unnoticed here.

Each and every one of you has a part to play in our actual environment, and I include discarnates in this. A recognition of this fact refills our flagging bread-basket. The basket simile is perhaps not too special, but one has a container which actually does flag and droop if Spirit is not uplifted, and the most basic earthly sustenance is in some form bread!

Please forgive my inadequacies in expression, but do not forget that each day is given us for a purpose, and do not forget that the purpose is not only to receive, but to give out, love."

—— ★ ——

3. Communication

First attempts, Building the channel, Using a pendulum, Telepathy, Acceptance of information.

This chapter describes how Peter set up the Communication Channel, which he summarises at the end. The communication technique between Peter and his father Michael is essentially 'Clairaudience' or telepathy, a form of direct mind contact with the discarnate person. Peter's mother June began with a pendulum and letter board, gradually developing the faculty of telepathy. The energy used is love.

First Attempts   21.8.87

"Dad, here is my first attempt at communicating with you by clairaudience. If you can sit down like this regularly, we will get somewhere. In the meantime do make a habit of sitting yourself regularly, and maybe we can build up the channel between us – Love Pete."

Building the channel   31.10.87

How the contact between Peter and ourselves was made:~

"Hallo Pete! How do you set about making contact?"

"As I said, I bring you to mind, and then concentrate (I have had to learn what is called 'superconcentration') on forming a channel down which I can send my thoughts. That's how I can sort of slide down it through the levels. No, the channel is of thought energy, sort of solidified. Difficult to explain, and as one goes into it there is a compression of ones range of thought, making it more difficult to manipulate ideas."

Using a pendulum   15.1.88

"Mum is coming on well with the pendulum, and if she could just have a little more faith in what she hears, she wouldn't need the letter board. I find the pendulum method a bit slow compared to the way we are speaking now."

"Pete, how do you set about communicating, say, influencing the pendulum first of all at your end? You got Nona[1] doing it very well the other night, and I presume it can't be too technical."

"No Dad, one just relaxes, and thinks of you. That brings a part of us down to your level. Then we just wish that the pendulum swings in the certain way, say clockwise, and because it is so finely balanced and you have given it the initial push, the effort of the wish affects the muscles of your arm and causes the pendulum to turn clockwise. Difficult to explain, but no more difficult to do than balancing on a bicycle. Like cycling one sometimes falls off, or goes wrong at times, but on the whole one doesn't have to think about the mechanics of it once one has the idea and has used it a bit. Nona seemed to pick it up very quickly."

                                                        9.3.88

"Pete, your Mum made the point last night that all the folk who tried communicating with us had very little difficulty in working the pendulum quite satisfactorily. How easy is this from your side?"

"Not too difficult Dad, with encouragement. It is really the exercise of concentrating one's mental powers one-pointedly on getting the pendulum to move where one wants it to. This is through the involuntary movement of the medium's arm and hand, because you realise, the pendulum is so balanced it is very easy to swing by a slight jerk of the fulcrum. It's a sort of psychokinesis in a way. But, of course the ease by which one influences the medium, depends on how open the channel is between you and us, and that in turn depends on:

1. The medium's thoughts about us.

2. The medium's inate ability to be a channel.

3. Our thoughts about you.

4. Our abilities here to form a clear channel.

Once the channel is opened, as it is with you, the use of it is comparatively easy. Sorry to be so wordy."

1   See *Appendix of Names.*

35

COMMUNICATION

"We were wondering Pete, how it is that someone like the lady, who was on the channel last evening, and who has never worked the pendulum before, can straight-away use the channel successfully without help and assistance from you? In times gone by, we had the impression that you were there helping people who came fresh to such a communication technique."

"The reason lies in the way the channel is set up at this end. It is now fully established firmly, and enhanced each time we think of each other, which is usually many times a day! Once June takes up the pendulum, the channel lights up. At this end all someone has to do is to think of the letters of the word being sent, or even just of the word as a whole, and the pendulum is influenced. So, little tuition is needed by most people, particularly if they have a strong will to communicate."

"What safeguard is there to prevent an undesirable spirit from taking over the channel when you are not there?"

"Well, to start with my *influence for the good* remains with the channel even when I am absent. A person using it has to have my blessing to do so, otherwise they get nowhere with it. Secondly, you put up a guarding prayer at your end, which each time helps to strengthen the restriction of use to desirables. I will try not to be away when you sit down for communication, but cannot guarantee it in emergencies."

"We have discussed this before Pete, but what exactly does your end of the channel consist of? One can imagine a desk like a Radio or TV studio, with microphones and cameras, or a tunnel between us down which you peer, but I am sure it cannot be anything like that!"

"No Dad, there is no desk or camera or microphone. Just a rather comfortable sofa or chair, on which the person communicating sits. The channel ending is an *area of thought* about yourselves—and here thought has a solidity not experienced on Earth—in which the Communicator immerses him or herself, and through which, by will, the pendulum is influenced.

It really is right manipulation of thought, and some people have difficulties with that at first. Others who perhaps have tried it on Earth take to it very quickly. As I explained earlier, there are various safeguards on the channel to stop unauthorised persons, (unauthorised by me) using it. Does that help?"

"Yes, thank you Peter. No doubt I shall become familiar with it when I eventually arrive with you. Mum was suggesting that most people arriving in your area Pete, are too taken up with new experiences to care much about the details of their past life and death. So, when their friends and relatives here ask for details to identify them, the deceased have some difficulty in supplying such details. Added to which there is this temporary amnesia we mentioned."

"Yes, this is so. Past life details are irrelevant when one gets here, so unless the love pull is very great, people here have little incentive to think back on such details."

Telepathy 4.1.88

During January 1988 we discussed Telepathy on a number of occasions. It was suggested that June's telepathic abilities might become more fluent with practise. Peter thought this would be a desirable improvement over the pendulum:~

"I think if Mum can practise telepathic communication, perhaps with the aid of the pendulum and letter board, several times a week as suggested, it will not be long before she gains a fluency in the method, which will please us both."

"Well, what about our telepathic communication, then? How does that work?"

"We project a thought down the pathway formed by our longing to communicate—*thoughts are real energy* you know—and provided the channel is clear, you receive our thought and translate it into words, and in your case, write it down. I prefer projecting thoughts as we are doing now. Of course, for people who advance beyond this sphere, it is sometimes more difficult to form a channel. They have left this level behind and find it sticky to pass through, and have further to go to reach Earth level. So, unless the pull is very great to communicate, or they pledge themselves to do this work, they tend not to communicate so often. That is why most mediums pick up people who are at this initial level, and unless they have been to classes and worked hard, they don't know much more than they did before they left Earth!"

20.1.88

"Morning Dad! I do hope Mum improves her telepathy, 'cos I find the pendulum a bit exhausting after a while. She can see how fluent one can be from our short conversation."

"I think she is getting better Pete, but it takes a long time to build up confidence to grasp that what one hears internally is not always ones own thoughts."

Telepathy — a summary   24.8.88

"It requires an act of faith to dispense with the pendulum altogether. The crux of the problem is knowing that the voice in your head is the communicant's and not your own! There is a sort of feeling about it, and one eventually knows for certain, but at the start it does require faith. It is not helped by occasional lapses, as when deciding what you think is being sent and finding one is wrong! Perhaps, the alternative is something you on your side thought, or perhaps it is a conclusion jumped to by my imagination. It does seem however, that if one is locked into the channel, the flow of words can be strong and continuous, and they are yours, not mine."

Acceptance of Information   24.3.88

"Many people won't believe in the continuity of life through death, Peter. They won't believe that our conversations are between you alive on the one side of the divide, and me on the other. But, because of the extraordinary clarity, they may well decide, privately perhaps, that both flow from my mind. What comments have you on that?"

"Well Dad, you cannot expect other people, who have not experienced anything tending to confirm life following Earthly death, to be as confident as you and Mum are. After all, the western view of death as final is very hard to shake off. Except for very rare cases, one only experiences it once in a lifetime! So it follows, the tendency may be for readers to be sceptical about our conversations.

Don't worry about this. Enough people will accept the information to make it worthwhile, and those who don't accept it at first will grow in time to follow suit. All one can do is scatter the seeds of knowledge, and hope the ground is fertile!

Of course the conversations flow from your mind! How else could we talk? The pendulum, or automatic writing *are* mind operated. So is Paul's voice box when he leaves his body. Each reader must decide whether the information I give you comes from me as a separate identity in another world, or whether you are in some way concocting it all. Perhaps, there may be some evidence tending to confirm one way or the other, but basically it is a personal decision of the reader."

Summary

Communication between the levels of existence in which we have our being exists. It is faith and will that transcends doubt and fear:~

"Communication between Earth and Heaven is one of Life's mysteries. So be it! The essential truth is that it exists! Perhaps, people are confused by the varied ways experienced, there is no Blueprint to follow. For some the communication consists of a distinct, but unknown voice, in the ear. Complete realisation belies scientific evidence, yet the receiver knows. For others, communication can be a voice in the head, a subtle, and inexplicable difference. Some see images, and are aware of their meaning. Others find they produce writing independant of their control. Yet others have a direct telepathic contact, and for others the pendulum is the point of contact. The reason for the variation lies within the complex world of energies, and the matching of vibrations. I do not intend to enlarge on this now. I only want to stress, all these processes are a facet of one truth: *We are all energy vibrating at different frequencies, and once our frequencies are matched, there is no divide."*

Editors' note

Communication should not be attempted by the novice without the presence and guidance of an experienced sensitive, or without raising one's consciousness to the highest level attainable through meditation. There are many low level and negative entities in the Astral world waiting for a chance to jump in and take over an open mind. Peter's channel is closely guarded. Love is the key.

4. Manifestation

Peter attempted to appear on Earth to a small circle in his parents home, hoping to prove in this way the continuity of the incarnating spirit. He began with a series of attempts to transfigure a medium. He subsequently recognised that to manifest as a free standing spirit would be more desirable, yet beyond his own powers.

He explains the process of manifestation and materialisation in his summary, stating that we base our assumption of existence, at any level, on its 'wavelength', and that when we die, for instance, we are simply transferring our existence to a higher vibration.

First attempts   4.9.87

"Hello Dad. Well I nearly made it last night, didn't I?. Then we realised we hadn't got things quite right. Perhaps we can try again next week. Energy for materialisation is about two to three times that needed for just talking, so talking is more economical. You would like to see me again wouldn't you? I'll try again soon if they will let me."

10.9.87

Attempting transfiguration:~

"They say I am too young to do this, young spiritually that is. But, I want to make my presence felt. Tell me whenever you feel anything, or see anything..."

The medium's profile was seen to change, together with size of face and hairline. Eyes were seen blinking above those of the medium, which were closed, and a smile appeared.

"Are you happy?"

"Of course we were."

"I am going ahead. Trying to do better, and want to be clearer..."

25.9.87

"Sorry about the fiasco last night. We tried three slightly different ways to control things, but were not successful. One has to control the power in such a way that it manifests according to the mental memory of one's earthly body, sort of gels together. Better luck next week – Peter."

8.10.87

"I am just going to try and descend... to come down, come down, come down, come down... right down to your level. I want to put every effort into it, you understand. Send out positive thinking.

I am not sure that it is going to work, but as I come down it is not going to be all that easy to talk. So, I might go very silent. What I need is to hear from you all, whenever you can be aware. Each of you will be used to draw energy from. A few more steps, and a few more steps. It is like trying to get to the bottom of a swimming pool."

(Outline of a face seen to appear).

"Strange, can't understand it. After the first attempt thought you'd see my body sitting here. I need to... at these levels. Strange physical body... also various fields round the body getting in a muddle. Doesn't feel normal to me. It's like it hasn't come as strongly as I really want. You see it's better that I try this with you because it is more experience, coming down, and I'll have a stronger link with you all."

15.10.87

"Morning Dad! Well it's today I hope... bottom or bust! I'll certainly be doing all I can to make it this time. Hugh[1] says I should put everything into a sort of dive, so my momentum carries me through. But, I don't want to make you all collapse by removing power too quickly, even if I could! Anyway, I'll try my best."

(*See 'Problems'*).

Use of colour   2.10.87

The effect of colour in matching vibrational frequency between spirit and Earth planes:~

"Sorry about last night. We did try one stage of it, but things weren't right. Let me explain about the light. It is a matter of matching vibrational levels. I have to come right down in vibrational rate to materialise in Paul, and if he is suffused with red light it can

1   See *Appendix of Names.*

41

make matching my rate with his more difficult. But, we should have let him know when he chose the right colour. I don't think we appreciated quite what a difference this would make. You see colour tends to pull a person's rate to fit at the appropriate level, hence its use in Healing. Hope we have better luck next week."

"What about this lamp colour then, Pete. What colour should we use?"

"Blue, of course. It worked when I was trying to transfigure, and it should work now."

"Well, what are you trying to do?"

"I am trying to make an appearance through Paul, so you can see me as I was on Earth. It's not so easy though. Everything's got to be right. Not too many people have done it lately, and those that have, have moved on and can't be easily reached for advice. At least that is the team's experience.

Once we have done this then Hugh feels the contact between us will have been fully and truly established, and we can move on to other more important things, though right now I feel this is the most important work."

Problems   9.10.87

Difficulties encountered in manifesting, and the ways tried to overcome them:~

"Hello Peter! Well it was a pretty successful evening wasn't it? You made it almost completely down."

"Not as perfect as I want though. The last stage is more difficult than I thought. It needs more efficient use of the available power."

"What was the main trouble then?"

"I think it is just that. It felt most odd coming so far into Paul's body, and I found it so difficult to actually do anything when I was there. Sort of cramped up. I think I almost panicked. Have to stay calm. Now I realise what a lot of difficulty we live with on Earth. Hope to be able to try again."

"We are very interested in how you set about communicating, especially transfiguration, and your present manifestation. Is it purely a mental process, and if so how do you start?"

"Yes, well I'd rather not say too much till I've done it successfully. There are several ways to attempt it. But yes, it is basically a mental process. The medium makes a sort of channel, or tube of mental material into our area, and we use that. But, it needs someone of a wider experience, and high in consciousness, to help someone like me use it successfully."

"Is our conclusion correct that you are now looking at a different form of manifestation?"

"Well yes. There are several methods of doing this, and since my first attempts were not completely successful by the one method, I thought I would look at a different way. I am not at all sure that I can explain these in a way you could understand, though I seem able to comprehend the method intuitively. The method I was looking at last night involved putting the medium into a state which he found frightening, but this may become less so with practice. Whether we can use it depends on whether he is willing to take the risk of the sort of displacement involved."

"Are you regaining past knowledge in depth, or is it still far beyond you?"

"Well, a lot of things are now coming back which I must have known in the past, but were forgotten when I was born last. They are sort of dreamy feelings about things, but turn out to be true when I enquire. During the last session there was quite a team involved, with highly specialised technical knowledge. They just came together for the operation of demonstrating to the medium the way it could go. I don't know where they came from, or where they went to. Rather like a team of highly technical removal men!"

5.2.88

"Well, can you tell us what happened last night?"

"The idea was that the medium should come up to us."

"How does that differ from his usual trance state, and what was the tightrope about?"

"Usually, he just vacates his body, and goes off into the astral area somewhere. This new idea is that he comes up to our level, and the tightrope is symbolic for the narrow path he must tread. By doing so he opens a channel, which is particularly easy for one of us to use, into his physical body.

Last night the medium was not ready for the crossing. There is obviously a risk associated with this way, and the image of safety nets is one of our protection. Your bridge of love is one you can create from your side. This way has not been very much used in the past, and created a lot of interest here.

There is a danger of course, but so there is with just vacating his body. This way provides a dedicated path held open for us to use, by the presence of the medium among us, and an opportunity for him to be right among us for a period with the advantage of gaining improved knowledge of our area. We realise now that he must be better prepared, and seek his full cooperation."

"Do you think you are any nearer achieving full manifestation?"

"Yes, I think we are. It does require several conditions to be just right though. I think I have more experience now, having spent over a year. I would be prepared for the stickiness and strange feeling of an Earth body, having tried to come back before.

The last step into Paul's body was like going into a very uncomfortable dark hole where one is confined, like diving off a high board into water which may not be deep enough to cushion your dive! Needs a lot of courage! In addition the medium must be in very good health, and other conditions must be right. You are only a small group and the power is limited. We will try again and hope to succeed this time."

18.4.88

"Sorry you did not get further than halfway down last night Pete."

"Yes Dad, things became more difficult than I had thought. But, next time I will be prepared for this, and hope to get through."

"Did you have backup from your friends? I was not aware of the sort of power extraction from myself that I experienced with some of your earlier attempts to manifest."

"No, that would not be necessary as I approach your level of consciousness to extract energy from you. It was at an earlier stage in the process that I ran into difficulties.

Imagine sliding down a smooth tube reaching from my level of consciousness (I say this 'cos it's not 'physical levels' I am talking about), to your level of consciousness. It's a thought process. Then, after a while coming to a rough bit of tube which impedes your progress. One either has to have more power to get past it, or some lubricant to get over the friction. That's roughly what happened last night."

"How do you set up this thought tube, Peter?"

"Visualisation and love, backed up by will, are the main ingredients. But, one needs practise to originate and sustain the image enough to use it successfully."

Summary

The experience of manifestation served to emphasise the continuation of Earthly characteristics. Peter explains what this means in terms of surviving death:~

"This is a subject very close to my heart. Manifestation is the ultimate in emphasising the continuation of Earthly characteristics. I find it difficult to understand how anyone experiencing a visible home coming of someone from the Spirit realm, can question our survival, and link with our Earthly selves. However, I am told that even this can happen. Hence, few are prepared to return in physical form. The effort involved both psychologically, and in terms of concentration, is enormous for a newly installed discarnate.

'If proof is regarded as vital, why bother?', they say here. Plenty of manifestation has taken place in the past. Seances were geared to physical phenomena in the early part of the century, yet still proof is considered lacking! Now, a lack of commitment by recently incarnated mediums to ectoplasm excretion, has meant that alternative demonstrations must be evaluated. Hence, my own efforts have been directed with alternatives in mind.

I want to try to describe my experience: I have endeavoured to transfigure a medium with a degree of success. I have decided the more impressive achievement would be to manifest as a free standing source of energy. Let me explain the difference.

To transfigure in a manner that leaves no shadow of doubt, or perhaps no doubting shadows, in the minds of the perceivers, not only demands both Spirit and Mind to vacate the medium's body, but demands also that the incoming Soul shrinks, so to speak, in order to crawl into a constricted area. When I tried this I literally panicked! It was so dense I felt frightened, and could do nothing to aid formation of my own physical form. I wanted effectual escape to what has become an intensely comfortable situation, in terms of consciousness. I know that with experience I could learn to contain my reaction.

Much deeper understanding of vibration rates would assist me now, but I feel for the medium, who is trying to put total trust in love and knowledge of our good auspices. Perfect trust is vital, and is totally necessary for success.

How many of you would be happy to vacate conscious grasp of a familiar scene for a few moments. In meditation for example, you are able to return at will. For the medium committed to loan of body, the return can only be made when the incoming Soul moves out. One is handing over one's own designated homestead. Control of it, albeit temporarily, no longer belongs to you. A complete stranger is living within it's confines."

Different planes, different vibrations

"I have given a constricted look at the process of transfiguring a medium. Now I would like to try to explain both manifestation, and materialisation. They are not identical processes.

I have a desire to be seen as a solid entity because an experience of this nature should make it possible for anyone present to shout the news of survival from the roof tops, and it is my understanding that the universal acceptance of survival is a genuine need of humanity at the present time.

Stop for a moment, and sit back comfortably in your chair. Put down this book, and give just a few uninterrupted minutes to consider exactly what life means to you now, and what it would mean if you were satisfied beyond doubt that annihilation at death, radical proposition that it is, had been disproven. That try as you might there was no escape! Into eternity one must step, and one's loved ones, and one's less beloved companions had all got to face eternity together.

How, I wonder, would you alter your behaviour? What would become of your ambitions if such a premise became public opinion, supported by governments even, the acceptable mode of thought for thinking men and women?

If you think seriously about the implications, it is my belief that priorities would change throughout the world. My materialisation will not by itself change the course. An intrusion such as this into major issues is unlikely to meet with everyone's approval. But, from small beginnings grow immense corporations. Help me to lay a foundation stone by not dismissing my bid for good instructive impact on some of the open minded amongst you.

Like most Earth inhabitants you will term materialisation to happen only if you find the handling of an object to be identical to the handling of your favourite piece of china, or the appreciation of your cat sitting on your lap. You are prepared, I am sure to concede that both are solid. They are of solid material, and can be handled, though at times both can be removed from sight. You are also prepared to believe that out of sight, though not necessarily out of mind, they both continue to have a real and individual identity. Usually, people fail to ask themselves what is meant by this identity. I suppose you would say,

'Well, they have their same form, though I cannot see them now.' That assumption depends entirely on you *retaining in your mind* the vibration on which they depend. Should you, or they themselves change the wavelength on which they resonate, the image would disappear. That is precisely what we do on so-called death. Hence we no longer see each other in the same automatic way. One, or both, of us must bring about an altered state of vibration so that we once again resonate on the same frequency.

Now, if through meditation you are able to raise your vibration to a different intensity, and at the same time, we here, lower our vibrational rate to the slower beat of yours, 'Hey Presto', we can relate as you all do on Earth, and we all do here amongst ourselves. So you see the theoretical requirement is potentially plain. It is the execution of the combined effort that presents the problem.

Most earth folk give minimal time to meditation. Question arises of a dedication *on a regular pattern*. Unless this happens, the chance of reaching the high point seldom is achieved. To combine the experience with one of us demands total commitment. Do not think that we fail to seek opportunities. The process however, is subject to much depletion of purpose, on account of lack of speedy results.

If you are unable to raise your frequency of vibration, then it remains for us to lower ours. You are conscious of the fact that in any earthly project, the going can be doubly hard if another participant fails to meet you half-way. The concentrated effort is reserved here only for very exceptional purposes, and hence seldom reported. In such exceptional circumstances can be placed the rare occasions when very recently departed loved ones are briefly seen. I am calling this 'manifestation' a one-off gimmick, often the term engaged on such occasions. After all they are not usually repeated. They are the result of an incarnate's love and sense of desperate need, or the determination of a more developed soul to get over an urgent message. I want you to realise that in talking of materialisation, I am speaking of an occasion when a contact entails exchange of greetings, friendly discussion, and the ability to achieve the same relationship at will.

But please do not dismiss the possibility because it has inherent technical difficulties. Those who succeed on Earth generally have had the determination to get to grips with the problems facing them. If such determination was applied hand-in-hand with behaviour hostile to our existence being no longer promulgated, but a more positive attitude of enquiry taken by using the method of meditation—hence stilling Earth folk's stressed minds—realisation of 'more 'twixt Heaven and Earth' would soon be appreciated as valid!"

5. The Key to Truth

Philosophy, Making the most, Reincarnation, Past lives review, Soul and personality, Holy Grail, Handicap, Growing up, Experience of God, John Brown's body, Organ transplants – Man's interference, Choosing parents, Abortion and birth, Plan for life, Love energy, Anniversary, AIDS, Need for love, Sin and self-interest, For the joy of it, So what is Truth, Knowledge, Scientific view, Beliefs, Advancement, Attitude, Appearance of form, Of mice and men, Energy, Earth as sentient being, Rescue work, Teachers and Guides.

Philosophy

Philosophy comprises Man's wide perception of the World around us, and provides a basis of wisdom. This chapter deals with general truths as perceived by Peter:~

"I must not impose my belief that Psychology is a mainly misunderstood, apparently high profile subject at the present time. This may well not be so in future. It suffers, at the moment, from an assumption that a person's mind is the key to behaviour, rather than a link through which the Soul can express itself.

I must draw your attention to the much more ancient science of Philosophy. I know at present it tends to be associated with ancient theories and political concepts. Rapport with such a subject is considered to be for specific folk who dictate politics, be it World reform or local activities. A subtle influence is often termed 'philosophical' in essence.

Philosophy is in fact an ancient art, and expresses Man's wide perspective of the world around him. It has been practised for aeons of time, and has enabled Man to express the broad conception of his hopes and fears.

In preparing you for the revelations in the following pages, I want to try to awaken in you a wonder, and also an awareness of how, in days gone by, you too probably based your hopes and fears. I refer to the faith by which Man originally estimated his chances in both his Earthly life, and the more permanent hereafter.

I trust an opportunity may present itself, as you read my words, to put back the clock and restore that faith. A good deal depends on understanding the essence of life itself.

I realise that modern philosophy is based on an assessment of ideas formulated after studying philosophers of olden days. Indeed, much wisdom percolated through independent thinking men of those times. Little that can be described as truly original now stems from thinkers of the current age. They adapt a good deal of the ageless wisdom to fill the need for explaining present day values. I tell you, Truth has not changed. Values have altered, because Man now feels he decides consciously, mostly in the light of scientific knowledge, how the world should be managed, and indeed feels that eventually he will understand how it was formed, and the science responsible.

Our philosophers of ages past, on whose theories Man's formulation of concepts are based, had no knowledge of this kind. They studied the outer fringes of our galaxy in as comprehensive a way as they could, and gave to the World the most ancient of wisdoms; that based on the stars and planets. Their concepts were formulated through personal knowledge of Truth, and translated into something that the 'Masses' could see for themselves. I have to point here to reincarnation as a fundamental truth which enabled the philosophers of whom I speak, to have much wisdom in their Souls. Not all their statements were accurate, but basic concepts led to their understanding of Humanity and its troubles.

The Ancient Wisdom is no longer the prerogative of philosophers. It is understood by many whose Earthly path is of a totally different nature. I must not give the impression that Truth is no longer known to Mankind, but the great majority have lost appreciation of the basic concepts that are to be found just the same as before. A genuine study of Astrology as a discipline and its true comprehension will reveal the key to Truth."

Making the most   14.10.87

"Hello Pete! Have you a message for the group?"

"Wisdom from the other side, as it were... Well, I suppose the best thing I can say is: 'don't fear death, look forward to it, but try and do one's best to make the most of one's experiences on Earth.'

It seems it really is a privilege to have a life on Earth, like being allowed to dive around in a very crowded swimming pool, and far too many of us do not realise this 'till we return here, and consequently don't make the best use of our life.

'Help others, and try to protect the Earth's environment so we don't foul up the water of the pool that we return to.'

Anyway, those are my thoughts at present. Pete"

Reincarnation   9.1.88

The need for serial existences, and the constitution of man, his soul and personality:~

"Now you have been over some 10 months Pete, how do you view things, and how have you changed?"

"Well, to start Dad, I think I have a totally different vision of life now, as just one episode in a continuing serial of existence, which consists of many Earth lives linked by periods in the worlds I am in now. No that's badly put. It's really the other way round. The continuing stream of life takes place where I am now.

But, here one need not extend oneself at all. One can just live an infinitely easy life only too readily. So, periods on Earth are to give one the difficult experiences to balance up.

It's like being on a cruise ship. Most of the time one lounges in a deck chair in the sun, with every comfort. But, sometimes one enters a foreign port, and goes ashore to meet difficulties, speak a foreign language, and work through foreign customs. By the time one re-embarks, one is quite glad to be back in the familiar comfort of the ship, until another foreign port is reached.

But, one looks back on the experience of being ashore—how one got on with the natives—and can recount tales of one's adventures. One learns from one's experiences. I'm well re-embarked at present, no other port in sight! Actually, I'm starting to work through the experiences of the last life. Tell you more about this another time. Pete."

Past lives reviewed 23.1.88

"How are things this morning?"

"Very comfortable. I feel bathed in this warm light, just reclining here. No worries, except what I will have to repeat on the next lot of the review! Then, I get great support, no criticism, from the presence that is with me. I would just like to kick myself sometimes, doesn't work so well with a thought body!"

"Still Pete, this is the whole point of a life on Earth isn't it? If one doesn't make mistakes, one can't learn."

"Yes I know that, but I seem to make such large errors. I wonder why, now!"

"Well the errors were not totally yours Pete. Others must share the responsibility by causing the situation to which you reacted."

"But it's the way I reacted that counts, and that depended on the way I looked at events that went before. I see that now. I see also an echo from previous lives when I reacted in a similar way to similar events. My attitude changed when I was thrown into the Steiner school, in a world that was so different."

"You were reflecting the attitude of the world around you. Well, it is always hard to swim against the stream Pete, even if that stream is throwing you against the rocks."

"The best decision I made in that life was to go to the Steiner Schools, and I think that came from my higher self."

"Well, you made it didn't you?. That's what makes your life so very worth while."

Soul and personality 27.1.88

"Morning Peter! There are so many subjects that we would like to know about concerning your world. Perhaps I ought to list them. Can you confirm that the ideas we have of the real worlds are essentially correct, though details may need to be revised?"

"Well, yes Dad. What I picked up from those early talks we had seemed strange at first, but most of it has been confirmed since my arrival here. The details depend on how one looks at things. So much is subjective, and not objective, but the basic facts are:

1. We are an entity based over here.

2. We send down part of us to Earth to gain experience.

3. This part—the emotional and mental bodies controlled by the Soul—inhabits a physical body.

4. This physical body is built up in form and material by the 'plan of the Soul' working through the emotional and mental areas thus affecting the physical/etheric body.

5. This build up commences at gestation, and continues through birth by means of material from the mother's body, and after birth by the minerals and hydrocarbons we eat, to form the physical body.

6. At death we ditch the physical, and return (unless we get stuck at Earth level) to the Spirit world.

7. This is our 'real' world, our home, so to speak, where we continue growth and refinement, ad. infinitum, reincarnating as necessary to further gain experience.

8. This picture implies control of the Earth life by the Soul, but, in practice, this rarely happens at present, and the Personality bumbles along through life tripping over the rocks as it goes, often falling by the wayside!

These basic facts are correct, as far as I know them. Will tell you if I learn anything different – Pete."

The Holy Grail   20.3.88

"The Holy Grail is the mysterious quest which King Arthur's knights sought, and you may remember the story of Parsival who found the Grail within himself, by asking the right questions of the right people. The Grail refers, of course, to the accumulated experience of one's past lives as contained within the Spirit, and as shown by the colour vibrations to be seen by a suitable sensitive in the chalice-like head aura of the being concerned. Hence, the reference to the Grail cup.

These colours can be interpreted in terms of one's past experiences, which is what they are due to, and the aim of all Souls should be to attain the aura of the Christ, which is the true Holy Grail. For us all it is a long hard quest, but each reincarnation brings us, or should bring us, nearer to the ideal, by very slow degrees. It is not 'till one reaches a certain stage of awareness that the quest or it's object becomes known to the consciousness.

Here, one can see easily how far each has gone on the journey towards the Grail, and for some the journey has barely started. It is the job of those who have achieved a little awareness to point their brothers towards asking the right questions, and receiving the experiences that follow – Peter."

Handicap 3.4.88

"Do you feel you have 'moved on' since your arrival in your present world, over a year ago, Peter?"

"Yes I think I have changed a bit, quite a bit, but towards my true Self."

"Of course, had you remained with us you would have matured from the age of 17 to 19, so is your present change different to that?"

"Well, maturing usually means, I suppose, becoming more set in one's ways, taking more responsibility for one's actions, becoming wiser. My change seems more like a return towards what one truly is, from a condition where one was less than the whole, the incarnate condition.

I think I said before that one incarnates only with those characteristics of the whole Spirit which are going to be needed for the purpose of that life. A sort of filtering process goes on before birth, a 'need to possess'. So, one is usually much less than one's true Self, a handicap during any one life.

The experiences one meets in living are not to be surmounted too easily, else why return to Earth life? It is only now that one realises what was missing, how much easier it would have been if the whole Spirit had gone down! Sometimes that does happen; then Earth sees a most remarkable being, but that being is imparting knowledge, helping others, lifting the Earth-level on his back! Such a being, for example, was Rudolf Steiner!"

Growing up 6.4.88

"Pete, what would you like to talk about this morning?"

"Levels, Dad. When I talk about levels here, I mean degrees of awareness, degrees of expansion of consciousness. This is something which is a property of the Soul and Personality, as the Spirit grows in experience. I have already said that only a portion of the Spirit's past experiences accompany the Soul on its journey to Earth for each incarnation, and that there is a 'growing-up' period after return here to full Spirit status. I think I am well on my way in this process, though it is difficult to see from my position here how far I have to go to complete the process. Not until that process of restitution is complete will I be able to judge what I lack in experience, (or how badly I went through a given experience), and know what will be necessary in a future incarnation. Not that I am looking forward to a future life on Earth with anything but reluctance! The world is in such a state, and no doubt will be worse in future years. However, under these conditions, I know now that experiences will be more traumatic, and more valuable to my Spirit.

Sitting here and philosophising will not provide the measure of experiences that I need to grow further. I have to eventually go into action again! However, I am enjoying the present life no end! Apart from missing you lot of course, though these channels of communication are a great help."

19.4.88

"There seems to be an ultimate limit to the age our physical bodies can live to, Pete. Why can't we carry on experiencing and learning down here, instead of having to return, not that I would want to at present, the way the World is going!"

"Well, I think you have answered the question Dad. Why do we have terms at school? Surely, because at times we need to consolidate what we have learned. The experiences crowd in on one, and one needs to sort out the information gathered, or we would become overloaded. Of course, at school the teachers are human, and need a rest as well! Our higher teachers have arranged that the physical body only lasts so long, even for the best pupil, who does all the right things, and looks after their body. We need to look at our experiences in a given life so that we can arrange for the next one to provide the experiences we lack."

Experience of God   17.7.88

"What is your experience of God and the Christ power?"

"God paddles both his canoe and ours."

"An intriguing way of putting it. Do you feel you are nearer to God on your side?"

"Not necessarily. Depends what stage you have reached. I personally am much more aware of him."

John Brown's body   17.8.88

"What's on the agenda this morning?"

"I want to talk about death and dying. With millions of people doing just that every day throughout the World, one might have thought that the process would by now have become so commonplace as not to merit much comment in the news. But, the news, if you examine it, seems to be made up largely of stories of death and dying, in one form or another.

Death is a front page story. Birth merits a poor showing. Royal births seeming the most popular. Yet birth is the most traumatic event one undergoes, and to primitive man just as mysterious as death.

Now if both were linked by reincarnation, a much more interesting story could ensue:-

'John Brown dying three years ago, has today been reborn as Linda Lane his niece!'

How much more interesting, particularly if there were details of why she was venturing into the World again, and what she hoped to achieve...

'John Brown wasted his money on horse racing, reducing his family to penury. Linda hopes (and expects) to marry a millionaire, and to have to account to him for every penny, on pain of private beating! Will she do it, this time round? No Betting allowed!'

The World, at present, is littered with the worn out shells of past personalities, mouldering away in the ground; many, in America, preserved in lead lined coffins, or in a deep freeze! The funeral industry thrives over there. What a state of ignorance! Would families mourn the loss of their Patriarch, with quite such an intensity if they knew he was sitting up there laughing at them, and planning to return next time as a Housemaid! Peter."

Organ transplants – and Man's interference   11.1.88

Man's interference with the course of life generates karma or imbalance, which will need to be repaid.~

"What do people on your side of the divide feel about transplants and the donation of one's organs?"

"Well, to start with we feel differently about death, as you know. We don't regard the transition with such horror as most people in the Western world do, but as a simple change which one has experienced many times before. So, there is the question of whether by doing 'spare part' surgery one is holding back what should be the time of death, extending life by free will.

This may be okay if the purpose is to live a life dedicated to a useful purpose, as, no doubt, many such patients do. But, it is really the reverse of the coin to suicide—ceasing life by free will—which is rarely right, and often means a quick return to face the same difficulties which caused the suicide again. Actually, if the suicide is really loss of life to save someone else's, and provided the motive is good, this may be acceptable, but, it is man's extension of life, not God's!

The other difficulty with spare part surgery is that each of us has our own characteristic rate of vibration, our own 'note' or frequency, which is the combination of the notes of all our organs and parts. Now, if you introduce an organ which grew from an etheric vibration rate different from the vibration rate of the body it is put into, firstly it will either be rejected, or if this is overcome, it is going to have to learn to fit in with the new body's vibration rate.

Where a heart is involved, the permanent atom[1] of the donor is put into the host, and this can cause problems of identity, - the donor lives on in part, and is kept back on Earth when he should be free to develop over here, and the host's identity is in doubt! Pete."

Choosing parents 4.2.88

"Mum was asking yesterday whether all children born on Earth choose their parents?"

"Well, as I understand it this is usually the case. There may be instances where someone has to return to Earth unwillingly, in which case a higher being will assist in choosing parents for a suitable life. This is rare however, and usually when the decision to return has been made, a period of intense activity using access to the akashic record, results in prospective parents being located.

Remember however, that all have freewill and there is many a change of heart at the last moment particularly these days with the advent of abortion. The change in the law on abortion particularly concerns us, though death at an early age means another attempt has to be made. Thus, to us life as a baby is particularly precious because, despite the increase in opportunity, there is a corresponding greater loss at an early age. Someone who aborts at any age has to balance karma."

"What do you mean, Pete?"

"Well, in destroying life, even if that life would not be viable if it were born, men are trying to emulate God, and alter the natural course. On the other hand, if by doing so the mother's life is saved they have altered the course of her life, and this may be good or bad

1 Read 'The nature of the permanent atoms' in *A Treatise on Cosmic Fire* by Alice A. Bailey.

karma. Usually, on Earth, they don't stop to consider the implications of their action, and assume the life of the mother to be more important than the life of her child. This is not necessarily so, and perhaps the mother had been meant to transit in childbirth.

Beings arrange to die in certain ways, and at certain times. This is part of their life experience. If by freewill on the part of someone this death is averted, there is a karmic debt incurred. This may be good or bad, positive or negative. For instance if someone steps in front of a speeding car, and the driver by skill avoids hitting them, strangely enough, because the course of that person's life has been altered (saved in Earthly terms), a karmic liability may be incurred by the driver. I say may be, because the intent of the driver may ameliorate the situation.

Avoidance of death, the 'saving of life', is not always necessarily a good act. It's not without its perils. Even the substitution of another death, as when one person sacrifices their life for another, has karmic implications, good or bad, positive or negative. It is all very complicated – Pete."

Abortion and the birth process   28.4.88

"Morning Peter. Oh, yes! One of my patients, asked for your views on abortion. She is particularly interested in when the foetus is entered by the human spirit. At what stage in development?"

"Well Dad, the teaching here is that as soon as the egg is fertilised these two living cell groups start to prepare for the arrival of the soul. They each have cell consciousness which combines to form the vehicle for the life. The subtle bodies then descend. First the new etheric body which takes over from the mother's etheric body the task of guiding the development of the foetus. Then the emotional, or astral body, which imbues the foetus, and finally the mental body. This all takes place within the first few weeks of conception.

So, abortion of the foetus within this period, whether naturally, or by human design, means that the Soul has lost its vehicle, and has to look around again for another opportunity. Abortion after the seven week period by human interference is murder, and may, usually does, result in a karmic debt payable by the people concerned. These people coming over here have to learn the hard way. It is a question of intention, and knowledge (or lack of it), which determines the responsibility they bear – Love Peter."

7.5.88

"It is no argument at all to say that to stop illegal abortions, one must allow more legal ones! This can never be defended. It stems from the lack of recognition that all souls are of equal worth in the sight of God, and the lack of recognition of serial lives. Adults today will be babies tomorrow! It is ignorance that is responsible for this attitude, ignorance and refusal to face the evidence of the past hundred years and more, which is freely available to all!

What it means over here is a greater reluctance to try for incarnation, consequently tending to hold souls back on their path. Also, a greater effort at re-education of the abortionists who come over.

I feel deeply about this issue Dad, because my natural mother could have had me aborted, but took the more difficult step of a normal birth, and reluctant adoption. So, I am the more indebted to her for her courage. Love Peter."

A Plan for life   23.10.88

"Yesterday you were talking about fate when I was with you. I am sorry to disappoint anyone who likes to shrug off their destiny on to a third impersonal cause. However, their destiny is the result of:

1. Their plan for that life.

2. Their freewill.

3. Someone else's plan for their life.

4. Someone else's free will,

or some combination of these factors.

You either determine your own destiny by your original plan, or by changing your mind, or someone else does it for you, whether you are conscious of these things or not. If someone else does it for you, they incur karmic liability on your behalf."

"*Well, what about geophysical events that may shape your destiny Pete, such as floods, hurricanes, earthquakes, etc.?*"

"Such events are known to be possibilities by the *higher mind*, or intuition, long before they happen, and are taken into account. Love Peter."

Love energy, an essential ingredient   2.2.88

The need for Love and caring for others on the Earth, and their present lack leading to crimes against Humanity.

"Hello Peter! Well, what's the subject today?"

"Question of caring. Why should one care for others, apart from the fact that this is one of the Christ's commandments? Well, here one comes to realise that love for all others, regardless of the particular facet of human characteristics they represent, is equivalent to love of God. For we are all of us a part of the creation of God, and if one hates a person for what they represent, then this is one part of the creation hating another part. This is like an illness in the body of God.

Now, this is not the same as hating what a person does. This may be very proper if that act, or way of living, is against natural law. So, I can hate Joe Smith's action of shooting his neighbour, and yet love Joe Smith as part of God's creation. Love and caring is an energy which is essential *for the growth* of all living beings. It is as essential as Prana. In fact, I think it is a form of Prana.

It is in abundance over here, which is why people having a 'near death experience' feel the tremendous caring energy in this part of the Universe. It is less abundant on Earth level, and has to be drawn down and distributed around. If there is no love, life shrivels up and dies. One sees this in the present state of the National Health Service. The caring is not, thank goodness, quite absent, but not so complete and life becomes difficult for staff and patients. With the help of love, *almost anything is possible*, provided it is within the law, or the life pattern for the person concerned. Here endeth another lesson! Pete."

3.2.88

"I have more to say on caring Love. It is of such importance in the Universe that one can say it is the basic driving force, the petrol of God's action. Without love everything would come to a standstill. The opposite of love, hate, causes war of one part against another, leading to destruction. The lack of love causes paralysis, each part ignoring the other, and leading to a foul-up of the mechanism of living. Love is the driving force and the lubricant.

So, please ensure that love plays the major role in your lives, and all hates are transmuted to love, not only for your sakes, but for the sake of the World. There is only a modicum of love in the World today, and it needs much more to survive.

You remember the Bible instruction to love one another? That is just as relevant today, and as necessary between the leaders, and the led of the nations; between nations, races, and all peoples. If that one instruction was followed, the Earth would be such a different place! As the place I am in now is!"

"It is wonderful to know you are in a place where love abounds, and where you can grow in the strength it gives you. Peter, we try to accommodate our feelings to the altered circumstances without allowing our grief to affect you."

"Yes, your emotions are very evident over here, being an area governed by emotions. Grief and hate, hurt us here. So, try to find something positive to love, as a part of God's plan, in every situation, and be filled with joy at life. This will help yourselves immensely, and others around you, and puts up an aura which delights us all here – Pete."

Anniversary   27.2.88

"Dad! I know the anniversary of my death is coming up, but please do not grieve for me. That only drags me down. Be glad for my sake that I have returned to this wonderful place. All of us over here, on this level, are full of life, sometimes fuller of life than we were on Earth, and happy. It only distresses us when those we love on Earth are sad and grieve. This emotion comes straight to us, and affects us immediately. Send us love, lots of love!

It is worse for those who cannot contact their relatives and friends on Earth as I am able to do with you lot. So many on Earth still seem to think of death as the end of everything. It is not, it's the start, or rather restart, of a most glorious life. One is so glad to be rid of that confining body, like a deep sea diver's suit, the old variety with lead weighted boots! So please, for heaven's sake literally, be glad for my death. Rejoice on it's anniversary, as you do on my birthday. The separation will not be for long, I can tell you, like the camping holidays I used to have, then we shall all be together again. Till then, send us love and happiness, and we will in turn, send love and happiness to you! Love to you all – Pete."

AIDS   3.3.88

"We hear of mothers with young children affected by AIDS. The mothers may die and the children need extensive medication to survive. What do you think about these situations?"

"The AIDS virus has been hovering round the Earth for a very long time, but it is only in recent years that it has been able to get such a hold, and it will spread until attitudes to casual sexual relationships change. We have had many aeons when this sort of act would have been regarded as contrary to religious beliefs and akin to rape. Now it is widespread and is the cause of yet another Earth plane experience. Yes, on the Earth level one can be very sorry for the mother and child in this situation. So unfair on the child! Yet, that child knew it was coming down into that situation; that mother knew at her soul level that she would return to us through that experience of sex. In my last life but one, I learnt my lesson of casual sex, and steered clear of it in this most recent life. There is no blame attached to the individuals, they have chosen to learn this hard way.

Doesn't it also show the awful fear their 'friends' have of dying through the AIDS experience, and the depth, or otherwise, of their caring for the victim? Over here, we welcome them back, the better for their experience – Pete."

The need for love   9.4.88

"Good Morning Peter! What's the subject this morning?"

"The state of the world! The lack of caring is horrifying to us here. People are treated like pawns to be sacrificed for the benefit of those in power. This is the same whether those in power are airline hijackers, or the present government, and probably most other governments as well when in power!"

"Do you think the position is any worse than in the Dark Ages for instance Pete?"

"In a way it's worse because the 'pawns' are now much better educated, and their sensitivity is roused. The peasants of the Dark Ages expected no more or less. Today, people expect a peaceful, helpful approach, and are more distressed by emotional power lust that takes advantage of their weak position.

I think I commented before that their position makes for rapid learning, but that in turn results all too often in violence. So many are returning to us now that our rest homes have to be expanded. Luckily this is easy to do with the etheric material of this world, but they have to be staffed by the right kind of souls, able and willing to help, and there are not too many of these. I toured one such home the other day, and the emotional injuries suffered by so many newly returned were only too visible. They need lots of love and caring by devoted staff, and time to straighten out the emotional damage.

Where there is karma to be repaid through their actions on Earth this is held over unless they are able to work through it here. Love is so often missing in relationships on Earth now, and the position seems to get worse year by year.

The only bright and positive signs are the increasing numbers of spiritually based groups that are springing up. They form a network of light, which will grow given time. Some are only dimly aware of their spiritual base, others are perhaps too spiritual, and insufficiently grounded. But, all make a much needed contribution to enlighten the world gloom – Peter."

Sin and self-interest   19.7.88

"I would like to talk about the way people act when they are given the opportunity to sin. Over here, as you must know, because of the very strong element of caring that is present throughout, people's thoughts are for the welfare of others, and not just for themselves. Thus, the sort of crimes which seem to be getting more and more frequent on Earth, crimes on the Person, and on the State, physical crimes, financial crimes, just could not occur here.

On Earth, too often, governments give the lead by hypocrisy and immorality. People at the top of financial concerns cheat the country of millions in swindles. Bodies that should represent law and order, like the Police, harbour rotten elements. Doctors act with inhumanity and a lack of caring.

In short, immorality, and a lack of care for fellow human beings is widespread with you on Earth. Children are no longer given the example they should have to model their behaviour, so it is little wonder that they tend to go the same way as the adults they hear and see in the world around them. I know I must sound like one of the ancient prophets of doom, but unfortunately it is true and immorality and crime are getting widespread. The reasons are a compound of greed, fear, and the feeling that because there is only one life, so the majority believe, and the only end is pleasure for the self, people must have all the material advantages that everyone else has. 'The World owes them a living'! Self-interest, and a lack of caring for others are at the back of all such behaviour. If they could but realise the continuity of life, and that they are on Earth to learn lessons for a short term, perhaps their attitudes would change. We must work towards an acceptance of this change of understanding of the purpose of life on Earth, or rather lives on Earth. I have a feeling it will be a long hard job to change attitudes of the majority, but we must try. Love Peter."

For the joy of it   28.8.88

"Morning Peter. Life seems rather complicated these days!"

"It's all a consequence of the emphasis on the material side of life, rather than the Spiritual. Everyone wants to get the greatest profit for the least work. That is, extract the biggest return from another person, for the least service done for them.

Wouldn't it be nice if people sold their houses for much less than the market value, or just gave them away to someone requiring that particular sort, and received a free house in return! If builders built just for the joy of creating a thing of beauty, as they do over here, rather than for the maximum profit as they do on Earth.

A fundamental change in human nature is long overdue. We need to return to love and caring between each other, rather than grabbing all the material advantages we can, to the detriment of our fellow pupils. Love Peter"

So what is Truth?   28.2.88

Truth and the subjective nature of the World. Each being has a slightly different point of view. As we advance, Group effort brings coherence of view and unity.~

"It's a beautiful morning here Dad, birds singing, a lovely clear light, and exactly a year by your time since I returned here. The Earth life seems almost in the dim distant past, though, if I concentrate, I can go back."

"What do you think of the description of your present world that I am reading at present?"

"Well, it seems pretty accurate, but you must remember that all of us see life here a little differently. And indeed it is slightly different for each of us. We are all, *at this stage,* different souls, and thus have different personalities attached. Thus, because this world is so subjective, it will appear differently to each. You know this to be the case to a limited extent with your Earth world. How the material world appears to a person depends on their past experience of it, as well as their present experience. Each will view it from their own circumstantial position, and interpret what they see somewhat differently. Thus, the view of the world given in that book is bound to be slightly different to the view each of us has here, but largely the same within limits."

"So, what is Truth?

"Well, remember that as we advance in these worlds we group closer and closer, losing our personal limitations, and the view of the group becomes more coherent and more clear, ('limpid', I think may be the term) until eventually, in the far distant future, a divine singularity of view is reached. That is the ultimate truth! All that we think of as truth before that point is reached is, more or less, subjective. Only God is totally, and by definition, objective.

This is why I urge you all to read books like Alice A. Bailey's *Ponder On This*, and others, that get nearer to the truth, in contrast to say a romantic novel.

The truth is not round edged and fuzzy. It is sharp edged and exact, often not very comfortable, but refreshing none-the-less. I now know that as I go up through the levels things around me will lose their warm, soft, comfortable appearance, and I shall be moved into areas of sharp distinction, of hard choice, where correct decision is crucial. My guide knows these areas and he has given me some idea of what eventually lies ahead. It sounds exciting, but mind stretching, – Peter."

Knowledge   23.3.88

Advancement in Summerland through Knowledge can be gained at classes. These are available to anyone who wishes to learn. Peter discusses the state of knowledge of the Spirit World, on the Earth.~

"Good morning Peter! What's this morning's topic?"

"Astrology. I've started to learn about this, at least the esoteric type, so called to distinguish it from the normal astrology practised generally on Earth, and not founded on the basis of esoteric knowledge; the 'As above, so below' principle is widely in evidence."

"We were very pleased to talk to Jack, our friend, last night. He confirmed that so many people in your area just sit around and don't do much. I suppose that is many people's idea of Heaven!"

"Yes Dad, only a relatively small number of us attend classes to move on in our knowledge and understanding. There is nothing to stop the others, anyone in fact, following suit. In fact they are encouraged when they do go, not criticised for their paucity of knowledge.

Also, it's free! Like everything here. The only 'payment' one has to make is that one must use the knowledge gained to help others. This is a natural law. Those with greater knowledge must use it for the good of others, and the Glory of God. And that doesn't mean the singing of praises about God in a literal way, but the maintenance of the 'good', and the spreading of Love, which is the energy that is God.

Action and service is the test of how well one loves God, action to help the good within the seven worlds (at this level, the lower worlds), and thus maintain the Will of God,$IWill;of God which is the will-to-good. This can best be expressed by putting the words of the 'Great Invocation'[1] into practise.

Sitting around doesn't do this, though when souls return here from Earth they often need such a period of rest or holiday to get over the traumas they have suffered on Earth – Peter."

29.3.88

"Good Morning Peter."

"Morning Dad. To know something, one needs to be *above* the level on which that aspect of the truth resides. Then, if one wishes for that knowledge, it will come into the mind by natural attraction.

No one can receive knowledge for which they are unprepared, i.e. knowledge which is resident at a higher level than the level of the mind which hopes to understand it. To see the reality of a truth sought, one needs to be above it looking down, and thus detached from it. Then, the pattern shows up as reflected light, or illumination. If one looks up from below, all one sees is a silhouette against the Divine Light."

3.4.88

"Love attracts knowledge. I may sin. I may lie; many do. No one is perfect. No one should judge another, except God! Peter."

5.4.88

"Knowledge must aid Man's quest for understanding his destiny. His many failings are the result of greed. Love transcends desire for measured calculation. Death proves that Man can ascend from a sense of amiability towards his fellow men, and learn to love them. Love to you – Pete."

Scientific view   16.4.88

"What is the subject today, Pete?"

"The way people today come to have some interest in our life here. It seems that for many it is a closed book, until something stirs them to open it. This is sometimes an enquiring mind dissatisfied with

1   The text of *The Great Invocation* is given at the end of this book.

what they learn from Science, or the Church's teachings, but more often the loss of a loved one, relation or friend, or a personal experience that cannot be denied. This is the case for so many.

Scientific dismissal of the possibility of life following death, and the consequent ridicule by the popular media backed up, for the religious faithful, by the church's attitude of interdiction—anathema towards mediums and their work; often portrayed as fraudulent or wicked, depending whether you are scientific, or religious, or both—has deterred many people who otherwise would have enquired further!

TV must take its share of the blame for presenting some biased programmes about the subject, which for some people only go to confirm that we are a figment of a vivid imagination. A result of a naive attitude to fraud! A 'Scientific' proof of our existence is demanded by some before our existence may be believed in, or enquired into in any way except with tongue in cheek! Yet, there is over 100 years of evidence about us accumulated by men and women of high repute, available to any who use their public library.

How much could the fear of death be removed, and grieving relatives comforted by a knowledge that death is only a transition into a greater life, and that some communication with those who have come to our side of the divide is possible!

I know how difficult, in the circumstances almost impossible it is, to provide a 'Scientific Proof' of our continuing life here. Difficult, or impossible, because Science does not encompass the world as it really is. It's basis in materialism is too narrowly drawn between high walls of rejection, and we are beyond those walls and thus rejected by all but a few.

It will change, and is already changing to a more moderate attitude Dad, but slowly. Perhaps, our channel may help in the process, that is why it is important to publish our communications as a book to try to reach those who have an open mind and an interest beyond the material. Love from Pete."

21.5.88

"Let's discuss the way in which true knowledge about the world and life is slowly percolating into the consciousness of the orthodox scientific materialist. It is very slow, and because it involves consideration of a system quite different to that taught in all educational establishments, schools, colleges, teaching hospitals, etc., it is bound at first to be rejected. Proof is demanded before any such ideas are even considered.

This, to the materialist means scientific proof, a very difficult thing to give, even in ideas which might be thought an extension to the orthodox, let alone such a radical departure from present teaching as we propose! Acceptance will not come this way. Radical ideas have never been proved before being accepted. Public experience has demanded fresh theories to account for the practical results. Marconi had to receive messages across the Atlantic, the Wright brothers had to fly, before the pundits would admit they were using the wrong theories.

The fact of the true constitution of man, and his serial lives, awaits the accumulation of public experience to force a change in materialist medical theories, not to mention the orthodox churches!

So it is all important to seize any chance of practical demonstration of the subtle bodies existence, and try to publicise it. It is bound to be rejected initially, any disturbance to the status quo of 'knowledge' is uncomfortable, let alone a change as radical as this! What professor of medicine will eagerly embrace a suggestion that he is only partially in possession of the true facts about the make-up of human beings? What absurd ideas!

Only through weight of public opinion, and the correct use of statistics will the orthodox establishment be forced to reconsider their present picture of the world. Even then they will try to force the new knowledge into the old mould.

The problem before us is that the body's fields will be accepted only as a result of activity in the physical, not as the means through which the physical form is produced and maintained. Practical demonstration of the latter through esoteric healing in these fields, will be necessary to show the true status of the fields. Peter."

Beliefs   2.7.88

"Today I would like to talk about people's beliefs, and the difficulties connected with them. People's beliefs are very often conditioned responses to their picture of the world, not carefully thought out conclusions from their experience. Thus, many of my friends have great difficulty in believing that I am alive, and are very sceptical about the continuation of life after death. Their picture of the world is based largely on what they have been told as a child and later, and what they have read.

Generally these days this is conditioned by the conclusions of Science. Medical science knows only about the physical body. It concludes anything as intangible as the mind is a product of the physical body, and therefore when the body is no longer alive, neither can the mind be alive. Thus, there can be no life after the physical body has died. Medical science is based on physical science, and most physicists believe they know all about the universe, and medical scientists believe they know all about Man, with only a few possible areas to explore. Most these days are as arrogant as the Victorians were in their model of the world.

There are a few at the top who are less sure, but this humility takes a long time to 'trickle down'. Thus, my friends will tend to reject any ideas that I may still live, whatever experiences of my presence they receive, because such a view of my continued life means a contradiction of what they have been taught, and what the majority around them believe.

It is very hard to hold views diametrically opposed to the majority. Any experience must be overwhelming to be effective, and it is in general more likely to be dismissed as an aberration of the mind. They don't wish to be thought mentally unstable!

Sorry about this outburst, but I am finding it very difficult to accept that my friends feel I am gone for good, and will not listen to my voice. People here did warn me that very few would believe. The deadening effect (no pun intended) of materialistic science is extremely strong, and difficult to reverse. We struggle on! Love from Peter to you both."

Advancement   1.3.88

A discussion of the advancement of the Soul or Spirit level compared to that of the personality of the individual.~

"I have read in Ponder on This by Alice A. Bailey, that the Astral plane is entirely illusion. Do you feel this Peter?"

"Well, do you feel that the Earth plane is illusion?"

"I don't when I fall on a hard surface! One has to try very hard, knowing scientifically that the solidity of material is an illusion, it is still difficult to believe."

"The Astral is partially like that, at this level, but the more advanced one gets in it the easier it is to accept it as all illusion."

"What do you define as advancement Peter?"

"The ability to see more clearly, emotionally and mentally; to regain knowledge more easily, intuitively; to differentiate between the important, and the unimportant things in life; and to put all these abilities into practise.

The result, a brilliant, clear, individual with an aura of love and caring warmth about him or her (gender at that stage is really not important)."

"And how far do you think you have advanced Peter?"

"There is a distinction between the individual at any stage, and the Spirit to whom he belongs. The Spirit may be quite advanced—part of an advanced group of Spirits—and the individual less so, if the requirement has been to experience a particular type of situation on Earth. Thus, when the individual returns, like the Prodigal Son, towards the Father, he has gradually to grow back to the level of the Spirit.

I think I am in that stage. It is like recalling all one used to know and value, bit by bit. Only when I am fully back at the level of my Spirit will I know how advanced I truly am, and how much more I must do to raise that level further.

So, I said to you the other day, that probably soon the surrounding woolly cosiness will vanish, and I shall be in a sharper clearer world. You remember how as a baby I loved cotton wool, the soft feel? Well, at the moment that feeling persists, but I know that soon that will have to give way to a clearer, sharper feeling that differentiates, that cuts through to the truth. That is the hard part to come, but the joy is that I shall know myself more truly, where I stand in God's universe. That's all Pete."

10.4.88

"The physical body and its needs are a big drag on one's spiritual advancement on Earth, or can be if allowed to take precedent over the rest of one's nature. However, since we need the physical body to live on Earth, and to experience all these lovely lessons, we need to take care of it and ensure it anchors us firmly to the Earth. No floating away into higher realms and abandoning the classroom!"

"But, isn't that what you used to do when young Pete, when your school masters thought you were dreaming?"

"Well, yes! That's why I'm pressing the point now. One should be stretched between Heaven and Earth, bringing down the best of Heaven to leaven the dull clay of Earth; the yeast to lighten the solid dough. But, we need the bread to live and grow in spiritual stature.

Do, both of you, use your time on Earth to advance your Spiritual levels. It is easier on Earth, in the classroom, than up here, to gain such improvements. Here, conditions are just too easy, and people just tend to relax unless they are very self disciplined and inspired. So I do urge you to read Alice A. Bailey's books, particularly *Ponder on This*[1] and others suitable. Peter, bye."

24.4.88

"Morning Peter. What do you want to talk about this morning Pete?"

"What we are aiming at Dad. The aim, as I see it, is to improve one's level of consciousness so that one goes beyond life as we know it here; so that we have no need of living in the manner we do, but step out of this into a higher life, leaving the personality behind, and simplifying ourselves to the Spirit alone. This doesn't mean to say that one cannot assume the garb of the personality if need be, but that normally one has no need of this. I think I have quite a way to go to reach this elevated stage, but it is something to aim at.

So many people around me do not seem to be aiming at anything. There is a feeling of excitement when I think about this aim, which seems to push me on."

"Have you been talking to Hugh[2] about this aim Pete?"

"Yes, we have had long chats recently, and he is very encouraging and helpful – Peter."

Attitude

18.3.89

"Good morning Peter."

"Love and caring for others is really the only energy that is of any value. People can learn many things. They can peg away at music, art, gardening, building or many other interesting things, but only for the love of being able to produce something that is beautiful, and can be given to others with love.

Moreover, caring for others with true desire to enable them to progress, is of the utmost value. I can only say that I know that those persons will always derive peace of mind, joy, and growth. I mean of course spiritual growth.

Some sit placidly, and no progress is made. Others question so much that they destroy their possibility of being actively involved

1   *Ponder on This* is published by the Lucis Trust, Suite 54, 3 Whitehall Court, London SW1A 2EF.

2   See *Appendix of Names.*

with giving. Their main achievement is to decide they are keen to reincarnate, so each time they do so they take back a little extra of the light from here. It is a slow business. On reflection, a large number of spirits must have done this many times. The consequence is that reincarnation is now a much prized event in everybody's mind who has something they want to master.

I said the other day that time is running out for Earth. No good can come of dreading the difficulties (of reincarnating). If mastery of certain concepts are needed, people must make haste.

On the other hand there is no room any more for those who are confused about purpose. Even experiencing deprivation is now at a premium. As starvation and death from earthquakes increase, the return rate will increase.

I don't want to be depressing, but it really is important that all problems are seen as experience, and progress in acquiring material things is given a low priority. I am not referring to acquiring material things that give other experience, or beautiful things that have been crafted with love. There should be appreciation of all beautiful things, not coveting for oneself, or for impressing others with quantity, or with the impressive manner in which one has acquired the power to get so much. I refer, of course to money.

Let these concepts be handed on to as many as will listen. I realise for many the propositions will be difficult to grasp. Perhaps, at Earth level the difference of which I have spoken is too subtle for some to understand. They may think of monasteries, and not having any possessions as the ideal. But it is attitudes that decidedly make the difference to what you do and have, not necessarily the action or the form it takes. Please, consider the difference. If necessary talk about this with me again."

"Alright Peter we will think about the subtlety of these comments and appreciate the aim. If your side is accepted at all, it is given more consideration than if it came from someone on Earth!

Appearance of form   9.5.88

In discussing the apparent solidity of the worlds we live in, Peter describes different levels of consciousness and the reluctance of peoples' acceptance of continued existence based on the 'scientific view':~

"Hello Peter. How do you view your body now, as solid and material as it appears on Earth, or misty and vague? And do you have the same sensation of riding in it, like a vehicle, that one can get down here?"

"Well Dad, I did say to you that at this level of consciousness things were quite solid in appearance and feel. So, it can be with one's body. But, you must also know that at this level things are not immutable. They can be changed by thought alone. This means that by thinking of my earlier earthly bodies, I can change my present body to one or other of them, so that people from an earlier life can recognise me again.

Etheric material is plastic and changeable by thought. Provided the thought is strong enough it will seem to be quite solid. Where the thought is not strong, it will assume a rather vague misty form. Now this is the same on Earth with material/physical substance, though it is rarely acknowledged. By thinking hard, some people can bend spoons, a rather useless occupation, but it illustrates the mutability of physical material by thought. It is not so easy on earth, the thought has to be stronger, and held longer, because the physical atomic/molecular bonds are also stronger.

In a sense one has to change solid into liquid for it to flow into another form, loosen the structural bonds. But, it can be done, even on Earth. So, how much easier it is over here!"

"Is there a preferred form that you assume, Peter, I mean, when you start thinking of a change of form, which one do you assume?"

"The form of my body in my last life is what I return to, but I assume the form of Charles[1] when I meet anyone from that life. Peter."

26.6.88

"I would like to talk about solidity. Some people seem to find the idea of the world that I'm in being as solid to us as the Earth is to you, rather too difficult to believe. Well, to start, one has to admit that what one conceives as one's surroundings on Earth is a picture built up from the input through the senses. What we think of as a solid block of metal is actually a construct of innumerable points of force each interlocking with the others: molecules, atoms, molecular and atomic bonds, crystalline structure and so forth. People accept that, since Scientists confirm it, it must be so.

Science is rarely wrong. But, in general, they still think of it as a metallic block, which is more convenient for everyday purposes. But when you leave the physical world behind with your physical body,

1   In Part 2, Peter describes his previous life as Charles Pizzey.

73

and come over here, you enter a world of mind and emotions, a world of the forces of thought, a world constructed from the *material of thought*, with the purpose of thought behind it.

The design of this world is the direction of the subtle material of emotion and thought into forms needed to make us feel at home, as we felt at home in the physical world. However, because of the fluidity of this subtle material compared to physical materials, the design may be changed more easily than designs can be changed on earth.

The design is upheld by our purpose for the time it is needed, and changed by common consent. While it is upheld, our world seems just as solid to us as the Earth world did to our physical body. But, when change is needed, the purpose changes, the material again becomes fluid and reforms into the new shapes we require, to become apparently quite solid again.

This process also takes place at the physical level with physical materials. Remember the spoon bending boys? Physical materials too can soften, bend and solidify under the action of strongly directed forces of thought. Science as yet has no answer to this except "fraud" and "hocus pocus", which, with the evidence presented, is scarcely adequate explanation! I hope this helps those who doubt. Love Peter."

30.6.88

"It seems that many people, probably most people in the Western countries, have great difficulty in conceiving that such a world as you describe yourself to be in, exists Peter."

"Is this surprising Dad, when religions have taught about extreme images of 'Heaven' and 'Hell' for centuries, or the alternative offered by Science has been annihilation! To find oneself in surroundings so resembling those one has just left, at least at a cursory glance, apparently so solid and peopled with ordinary beings, not clothed in white with large wings and carrying a harp, is quite amazing to most people. This is where solid, dependable, down-to-earth folk are invaluable to help the recently dead to accept their new life.

From where I sit I see the world as in great need of hope for a positive future on Earth, and beyond the grave, and caring for those souls in difficult circumstances. A shift away from the materialistic money grabbing attitudes that prevail is needed. These are really based on fear that there is only one life, and that can only be enjoyed if one has money. A change to an attitude that mankind can have a positive future by caring for each other, and that money should be used for the benefit of all, is urgently needed. Love Peter."

30.7.88

"There still seems to be a great reluctance with people to believe in our existence, or in the sort of life we describe. I really don't know how one can prove this, because people are now so used to accepting that things are the way Science says they are, and Science rejects the concept of life apart from the physical body. Or, at least the bulk of Scientists do. A few have a wider vision.

One of the reasons that the picture Science paints of the Universe is believed, is that using the scientific concepts technology has produced all these labour saving devices, like motorcars, T.V., fridges, cookers, etc. all through the "Appliance of Science". They are a fact! A hard, solid, physical pleasure-giving fact! Now, if the appliance of psychic knowledge were to produce better labour saving devices, (or even equally effective ones) such as dematerialisation, and rematerialisation elsewhere, or kettles that boiled without external power, adding more to the pleasure of mankind, then the concepts of life after death might be believed instead."

"What you are meaning Pete is that on Earth Souls have so forgotten their true home, and purpose in coming to this life, that they seize on any concept of reality which seems to give the best material results."

"Yes. For a long time mankind believed everything depended on the whim of the Gods. Then, that it depended on the will of one God; at least in the West, the East continued with the God family. Then Newton came along, and belief changed to his mechanistic theories. Now, we have a mixture of Einstein's theories, and Newton's, depending on the conditions.

At each stage mankind saw the prevailing theory backed up by practical results, or apparently so! Now if practical, material results could be obtained consistently using psychic concepts, life apart from the body would be the common belief."

"Well, that's all you have to do Pete, produce practical material effects consistently!"

15.8.88

"Hello Peter."

"I feel time is estimated in experience."

"The estimation of time as a life on Earth is associated with failing faculties, not necessarily accumulated knowledge."

"I know, the reason is few people think life goes on."

"Always did seem extraordinary more people have no inkling!"

"Became a bit less sceptical myself when I seemed to have so many bells ringing, warning of impending departure from Earth!"

"Yes, but many people can look and see they are having near disasters, but they go on for years."

"I think you would find if you analysed people's experiences that the difference would be that sometimes it would be recognised by the person that it was a brush with death."

"You are saying that if people were honest about their feelings, they would recognise it as a brush with death? A difficult thing to admit."

"People may not say what they felt at the time. I look at Earth folk only listening to communication by television, and pray some day they will think for themselves!"

Peter was asked whether he had encountered well documented people from earlier eras:~

"Cannot say I have encountered Elizabeth I!"

"Would she only appear as Elizabeth I to someone of her generation?"

"A lot of people have a link with past lives even after many reincarnations."

"Obviously one way they can recall is through records."

"I mean many other types of amnesia cause people to encounter groups from their previous lives."

"How do you appear to each other?"

"As we become locked into the experience we become those people."

"If you were sitting quietly reliving experiences of a past life, how would you be seen by someone arriving?"

"I would be seen as Peter, if he knew me as that, unless he too was thinking of the past life. Bye now."

Of mice and men   23.2.88

Light-hearted comparisons between the lives of certain small animals and those of human beings:~

"This morning I would like to talk about snails."

"Snails! Pete is that right?"

"Yes. A snail moves slowly and steadily, but still travels quite a long distance at times. It carries with it the accretion of its existence in the form of its house or aura, in which it rides as it were. As it goes it puts out its horns to probe what is ahead of it, to see whether it wants to experience whatever lies there, and behind it it leaves a trail from which anyone can see where it has been. Can you see that I am trying to make a comparison between the snail and the progress of the human being?

I believe too that, unpalatable as it may seem, the foot of God can, but very rarely does, step on our frail shell and crush us. Love for each snail prevents that happening!

One can carry the simile further by noting that some of us are rather slimy! Remember too, the snail's house which is a spiral structure. This is like our lives coming back to the same point, but hopefully more advanced each time round. So, next time you see a snail, think of the human being. Ponder on that! Love, Peter."

19.3.88

"Morning Peter."

"I would like to talk about mice."

"Good Heavens, what about them?"

"Well, you remember you rescued one the other night. That was a saintly act, particularly as that one might breed, eating you out of house and home! However, what I wanted to point out was that they represent the spiritual ideal in some ways: quiet and unobtrusive, industrious in chewing holes through wood, or chewing up paper for nests; also in social interaction, non-aggressive, timid, helping their neighbourhood mouse; knowledgeable and quick to learn in mouse ways, spreading the mouse word, or scent anyway. What a contrast to many humans! There should be a monument to the 'Unknown Mouse'. Love Peter."

2.5.88

"Good Morning Peter."

"This morning I would like to talk about hedgehogs."

"Hedgehogs?"

"Yes. You know the way hedgehogs roll themselves into a ball with prickles all over when touched? Well, some people seem to emulate this! Like a hedgehog they have a very soft sensitive underside, but a spiny prickly exterior, so unless one is very very careful and guarded in one's approach to them, there is no access to their nicer side.

Of course, this may result from fear coming from a previous bad experience. But, whether this produces the hedgehog, or the tortoise (retiring under a hard shell) syndrome must depend on other factors."

"Such as, Pete?"

"Such as whether the hard shell has deterred attackers in the past or not. I would rather deal with a smooth retired tortoise, than a prickly ball of a hedgehog, so the spines might provide a more effective deterrent!"

"Isn't this defence just a way of avoiding the experience, Pete?"

"Yes, but there is a strong tendency in all of us to do just that, where we know a bad experience is imminent. What we should do, of course, is to allow the experience to happen, to be open to it, but transform its effects on us from bad to good. This is not so easy to do, but is the desired way of dealing with it.

It is always the effect that an experience has on our emotional and mental sides and what causes it that is important, not the experience itself. How we regard what is happening to us, and what we deposit in our emotional memory banks about the experience. These are the things that count in the long run.

If, like the tortoise we just fend off the experience, it is likely to recur, and in a different form which can penetrate our defences, until we learn how to deal with it. Turn negatives into positives! That's all! Love Peter."

14.5.88

"Hello Pete."

"Hi there, Dad! Actually, this morning I want to talk about rats."

"Rats?"

"Yes, rats!"

"Well, we have had mice, snails, tortoises and hedgehogs. Now rats, Pete?"

"Well, rats are generally regarded with disfavour by most people, because of the damage they do by gnawing, taking food, carrying disease, etc. Though one writer at least, Kenneth Graham wrote in favour of them. I was talking to one the other day, and he was putting their case for survival. He argued that they were scavengers, and like other scavengers, birds such as crows, vultures, and animals such as hyaenas, they help to clear up the mess left by others, including mankind. This would otherwise be a breeding ground for disease. They did, he added sadly, provide a meal themselves, involuntarily, for foxes, and other predators. The reason that damage was done was because they had to burrow deep to hide.

Anyway, they were a balancing factor in ecology, and were better than some humans in the City, so he had gathered, who really did nothing but line their own pockets at the expense of the less wealthy. Rats lived off plants and food thrown away, and had a useful function in the world. Those humans, ugh!"[1]

"Makes me quite pity their lot, Pete!"

"Quite so, Dad! Must depart now. Love to all – Pete."

23.4.88

"What's the subject this morning?"

"Central Heating! Of course it is not necessary, but it illustrates various points I want to make. Because, heating emanates from one point, if something fails to work there, a boiler or pump, then all the heating breaks down. So it is with other human activity which depends on a central source. With local heating at least some of it works if one part breaks down.

Quite often an awful lot of hot air gets pushed out by the central source, and all the outlying heating units, or radiators, suffer. Finally, although central heating is supposed to be more economical due to savings in scale (size, not calcium carbonate!) this is often false reasoning because often one does not need all the building heated, only one part.

So it is with other human activities which do not always need to be carried on as a whole. This is an argument for Local government over National government. Over here, beings do their own thing while respecting natural laws, like caring for and loving others. Love Pete."

Energy

12.5.88

Solid substance is really energy:~

"This morning I want to talk about energies. Although energy is such an important part of our lives, it seems that only God knows what it is. At times it seems to be the basic building substance of the Universe; at other times, the means by which everything works to build, move, or live.

It seems that within the Universe you know, and the Universe that we know, there is only energy, and plans for the disposal of this

1   For communication by thought with animals, see also *'Cats'*, 6.1.89
     Chapter 7.

energy, God's and Man's. It seems what you and we take for solid substance is really energy locked up a bit.

Thought is energy; love is energy, the highest form we know. Energy exists in space, so where energy is not in space, there is Yang and Yin. God's plans also include Man's plans, because God allows man to act. But, as man becomes more and more destructive on the Earth, one wonders whether the divine foot will be put down soon! Or, is the ultimate lesson to be experienced by Man? These are just a few thoughts to Ponder On. Love, Pete."

Earth as a sentient being   4.3.88

The concept of Earth being an entity living within a larger entity:~

"This morning I want to talk about the concept of the world, the Earth, as an entity: 'As above, so below', as the Ancient wisdom says.

Firstly, this concept says that all things fall into a standard form:

1. A living being with a gross body, the latter being given form by a subtle field (or fields).
2. Energy Centres (7 is the magic number) on the being's spine, or equivalent, through which energy from the world in which it lives is concentrated, or transmuted, to flow at various levels through the 'gross body' to enliven it.

We see this best in the human being. The next entity up in order of size is the 'group', particularly the spiritual group; then the nation, then the world; the solar system, then the galaxy, and maybe then, ultimately, the universe.

Going down in size from the human being, are all creatures great and small, complex molecules, and atoms. There the analogy gets difficult to follow. If we think of the Bohr model of an atom, the concept of each entity living within the body of a larger entity is easier to comprehend; atoms living within molecules; molecules living within fleas; fleas living on us; we living within a group or nation; nations forming the population of the world, etc.

It is the structure of chakras—the energy centres of the body—that becomes more difficult as one goes up, or down, in relative size. I am assured by my teachers that the analogy holds good, at least at the level I am at present. The view changes as one gets more advanced apparently.

The comment I want to draw from all this is that we are indeed connected with all other beings, through the group, the community, the nation, the Earth; and that anything we do affects everything else.

We are not islands, but every action causes a disturbance, for better or worse, throughout the universe. Each flea bite causes us to scratch, and the country to tremble! So, we need to take a very much more responsible attitude towards our actions, and their effect on others, than is taken by most people today if the world is to survive! Bye, Pete."

Rescue work   17.3.88

Rescue work is one way of serving and helping those returning to life after death, those stuck on the Earth plane, and even those who return to the inner planes while asleep:~

"What's the subject this morning Pete?"

"Ghosts, Dad!"

"Good heavens, you quite scare me, Pete!"

"Why should you be scared, Dad? They are immaterial, and cannot harm anyone, unless someone opens themselves to the influence, but in any case most ghosts have no intention of harming anyone or being malevolent in any way. They are just the emotional side of a being stuck on the Earth plane and repeating an action they previously did so many times before.

Also, they can be with, or without a physical body. Ghosts of the living are probably as common as those of the dead, and occur where someone has an active obsession and leaves their physical body at night to repeat this action, which is often forgotten about when they awake.

Where the ghost is of someone who has died, we on this side, although I haven't taken part in this, have a rescue job to do to bring them from the earth plane, where they are stuck, on to our spirit plane; the sort of thing that Coco is doing.[1]

It is usually caused by the person having little, or no knowledge of the existence of the spirit plane. Consequently they are very loth to leave the Earth plane, even if they eventually realise, because they cannot attract the attention of anyone living, that they are dead. So, Coco's job is to persuade them they are no longer living, and that the best thing they can do is to go back with him. I believe he is very good at it too. Peter."

---

1   For examples of rescue work, see Part 2.

"Peter, I wanted to ask you for your comments on the idea that during sleep here, we leave our body, and return for work on the Inner Planes, as it is put."

"I haven't come across many of you sleep walking, though there was an occasion when I projected to Mum during sleep; that was early on, soon after my arrival here.

I think the point is that the bond between the physical and subtle bodies is much loosened during sleep, and the possibility of astral travel can occur, involving visits here, or at least up to a barrier beyond which we live. Though, unless one dies in sleep one could not cross this barrier.

A well intentioned person could help others during this period of astral travel, and there are plenty that need help, who have died and then become stuck at Earth level, the only level they know. In this way, some spiritual people could well assist those of us who go on rescue missions. In a way they would have an advantage, in as much as, if they are still alive, they can easily remain next to the Earth plane where these souls are trapped, whereas our rescuers have to make a dive into the heavier atmosphere of Earth to work. I will ask Hugh how much of this goes on during periods of sleep. I haven't personally come across any, but so far I haven't engaged in much rescue work – Peter."

Teachers and Guides   21.4.88

Peter's experience of spirit workers who can act as our teachers and guides along our soul path:~

"Good Morning Dad!"

"I was going to ask you Peter, whether to your knowledge, I or Mum had an 'orthodox' guide allocated to us from your side?"

"No Dad, I have the honour of that position."

"Well, I am sure you are very adequate Pete, and we love having your contact. But, during my healing work, I seem to have unseen specialists moving my hands, or holding them steady, or telling me when to move, etc. Do you play a part in this?"

"I am often there Dad, but you are right, there are Healers working from this side. They are rather more advanced than I am, and I don't know them quite often, or even see them. I just feel their influence going through to you. So, there is a team that comes into action when you start healing a patient. It doesn't just come from you alone, as you surmise."

"The teachings are that everyone has a guide on your side Peter, who looks after them, or tries to. Is that so in your experience?"

"Well, I can only speak for what I know, and that is that most people seem to have someone looking after them from this side, but quite often that guide looks after more than one person on Earth. Their brief seems to be to steer the person towards the experiences their soul desires, and the guide often has a hard job! I've met some of the guides at meetings and some of them despair of their charges, but still continue to try and steer them in the right direction, and away from material pleasures alone, with much love and caring.

The trouble is 'free will'. Everyone possesses it, and the pull of the materialist society in the Western nations is very strong. In other parts of the world the experiences are much sharper. Born into Ethiopia for instance, one is lucky to live to be an adult! A very hungry one at that. Material possessions, apart from food, play almost no part in life there. Life is stark, cut to the bone; you live on, or die!

Some souls need this experience at a certain stage of development. Others need the sort of reduction of life to essentials that being a hostage in a plane hi-jack brings for example. Like dying and recovering again. These experiences are conditioners of the Personality. After them the person is changed in their values of life. Love to you. Peter."[1]

3.4.91

"Good morning June."

"Hello Peter. Dad's asked you about the difference between Guides, and Guardians. Are Guardians always around, while Guides are not?"

"Really things are quite simple. Much is made of guides. If you think about it, a guide is someone who is constantly with you giving information. Whether it is a tour of London or a trip round the Universe is of little importance in assessing the role played. Consequently mediums will have someone on whom they can depend, for information on subjects that arise concerning spiritual matters.

It is a special relationship, and obviously the person is chosen because of not only the ability to open doors to our world, but because of empathy in terms of vibrations Their role will of course

---

1   A more explicit statement appeared in *LIGHT* magazine, Vol.III No.1
      Spring '91 entitled *Role of the Guide* by Chan.

have been embarked upon in knowledge that because the need would become obvious, the link might be made.

Like everyone else on Earth, paths can be mistaken following information, but those prepared to guide will keep in contact.

I feel that Guardians are people who love someone dearly. They are many in number, and have quite distinct roles, and at one and the same time they may be watching over many people.

I feel the link is love, and in the way of kindred spirits. Usually there is some past connection, even if it is from some time ago. The link remains because such interest evokes caring.

They try to help on all courses that life follows, but like on Earth warmer relationships both on Earth and here develop with contact, so the encouragement of being acknowledged will ever result in a deeper involvement.

Deliberately wanting support all the time is frowned upon. Have some thought for the Guardians' need too. I feel the real function is to befriend and support. Surely evidence for that role is totally comprehensible.

Life from here is not unlike Earth life. Do not try to find evidence for some indirect and unassailable role. Much love. Bye now."

Summary

Life is the instructor. Look at things around with openness, not with desire to advise, but with desire to understand. Adequate listening in meditation and contemplation will reveal the truth.

6. From Life to Life

Photos from a past life, Attitudes, A Planet fit to live on, The Easter mystery, Astrology as clue to purpose, Reincarnation in groups, Bird forms.

The fact of reincarnation is a cornerstone in the lives of many people who believe that evolution and the purpose of our lives are inextricably tied to the step by step, life by life experience of death and rebirth.

Peter discusses reincarnation, as viewed by those living on Earth and those discarnate, from the perspective of one's 'life plan', which he summarises at the chapter's end.

Photos from a past life   8.2.88

The discovery of a Victorian Age photograph album, which Peter claimed as his own when in his life as Charles Pizzey, (1860 to 1899, described in Part 2), started him identifying the subjects as his family and friends in that life:~

"What a wonderful performance last night, Pete! It quite amazed us that you were able to recognise so many in your last life from that old album, and give names most of which we didn't know! Well done!"

"I am pleased to be able to help, Dad. Actually, I have started to go back in lives, with that one being the first to look at – Pete."

Attitudes   19.2.88

Reincarnation is not always accepted by many people despite the celebration of Easter. The difficulties attending reincarnation:~

"What's the feeling about reincarnation on your side? Down here it is not yet accepted by any means. Some mediums say they have not had any mention of it from spirits they have contacted. Many others outside the 'new age' movement reject the idea. On the other hand it is a cornerstone of Buddhism and other faiths; more people are apparently accepting the idea, and there is a growing movement towards it."

"Well, as you know Dad, nearly all of us up here know reincarnation to be true. How else can one's lives on Earth be accounted for? There is certainly more than one life for everybody, many, many lives in fact. One has to be at a very high level to cease having to go back to Earth to learn. Maybe the spirits who said they did not know of reincarnation (or is it that they kept quiet about it?) had only just arrived here.

Actually, because being born is often so horrendous, some people here do not like to talk about it too often. People like to put off the time they have to try again at school. As you know in certain parts of the world, Africa, and India for instance, being born is being thrown into a world of starvation, privation, and misery. In the Western World, one sometimes even has difficulty in getting as far as birth. Someone reaches for you with a blunt instrument while you are still inside your mother!

No wonder reincarnation is viewed with some fear, apprehension, and horror, by many here. 'See you again soon' is in many people's minds when they know someone is due for rebirth.

I was lucky, (or was it really part of the plan?) with my birth last time. My natural mother might have had me aborted, but she was too well trained to respect life to do so. Love Pete."

27.4.88

"Good Morning Peter."

"And the same to you Dad!"

"Mum and I were very sorry to hear about Nona's troubles last night."

"Yes Dad, she is in quite a state about the possible loss of her friends and is not accepting the fact of reincarnation. This is not unusual here. People hide from the facts. The birth trauma is worse than it used to be by virtue of abortion, and the clinical, unloving way so many births are conducted, in Western countries.

People hide from the possibility of their having to be born again, by not admitting it to themselves. Yet, at some stage or other, we all have to return to Earth to advance much, and often there is much sorrow at the departure back to school. I suppose, birth is the nearest we have to the grief of a funeral on Earth. Peter."

A Planet fit to live on   14.3.88

"What is the subject this morning?"

"Well, I'll keep it short. It's interesting for people from the last century to talk to you, because although they can view the Earth world from here, they haven't incarnated since Victorian, or Edwardian times, and things have changed considerably. Attitudes have changed, and so have the difficulties people on Earth face. It could give them an idea of what they too will have to face when they do incarnate again.

Though the idea of going back again seems to horrify some, all of us at this level will have to continue returning. We just hope the Earth will continue to be livable. It seems quite possible that it will be difficult to support life. If people only recognised that they are destroying what they will have to come back to, perhaps there would be a change of heart, and governments would take more heed of warnings. I refer to the destruction of balances which enable mankind to exist on Earth.

But the first thing is the recognition that we do return in different bodies to live out different lives, and here the work of projects, and efforts to persuade scientists and medical men of the existence of the human being apart from his physical body, is vital. The rest follows. So keep up the good work, results are urgently needed – Pete."

The Easter mystery   2.4.88

"What is the feeling about Easter in your part of the Universe, Peter?"

"Well, like Christmas, it is kept as a religious occasion. The amazing thing to us is that, although, *in principle*, religious people on Earth (of the Christian religions) accept that Jesus of Nazareth left his battered body, and manifested in his subtle bodies several times thereafter, they won't take the exhibition of this truth, that we are not the physical body alone, and apply it to themselves!

This is the great truth that Easter should demonstrate, the use of a physical body for one life only, and the reality that life is a function of the Spirit, Soul, and Subtle bodies as the constituents of a human being. Hence, reincarnation for many lives for all but the highest of us.

This was accepted by the early churches, but thrown out. As you know today, this truth is not grasped by the majority, despite Easter every year! Love, Pete."

Astrology as clue to purpose 27.3.88

"Peter, to return to the matter we were talking about, your next reincarnation, we were studying the matter of your next reincarnation. It was suggested that it would be linked to Aries, and among much else that an incarnation in Pisces, which is the last sign of the Zodiac, was associated with clearing up unfinished business, and seeing clearly what was at the bottom of past experiences. The emotional side of learning, how to achieve inner peace. 'In Pisces one comes to help and give emotional support to others. Next time in Aries one comes with bluntness and purpose'. Do you agree with this?"

"Yes! I'm still going through past lives to see why, and to what end I had the experiences I had."

Reincarnation in groups 15.4.88

One of the factors governing reincarnation lies apparently in a 'group' with whom our purposes are often shared:~

"Good Morning Dad."

"Morning Peter. Interesting that you felt I was female in a life in Crete, which is what was said many years back in a psychic reading. I feel I have played a female role in many lives, maybe in the Washington one you have mentioned. Also, interesting that as a family we have been together on many occasions. I wonder whether this is usually the case with incarnations?"

"Yes, it seems to be, Dad. Talking to people around, they nearly all seem part of a group, or sub-group within a group, that incarnates about the same time, with a purpose to support, or chivy the other group members, according to the experiences required. This helps the other group members achieve their purposes in the incarnation, and if you think about it this makes sense. Other spirits, more distant from a Group member, would not have either the knowledge of the purpose of the incarnation of their friend, nor the same driving requirement to help the group as a whole by helping its incarnating member achieve. Thus, group members tend to incarnate together to provide mutual support, lovingly, or aggressively.

Things do change here if at a slower rate than Earth perhaps, and people advance, usually slowly. The fact is that advancement is generally quicker by going back to Earth experiences, than by just remaining here. But, not everyone is smitten with the advancement bug, and many prefer to remain here and work for a much slower rate of improvement, than return to Earth life at present."

"Does that mean that not everybody is forced to reincarnate?"

"Yes, there is no forcing, except by a soul's own mental pressure from the spirit. The drive to try again comes from each individual; probably via the group, who encourage advancement for its members.

Each individual has the choice, to go back to Earth and try to make a success of that life, or to stick on here, and by working hard try to gain advancement more slowly – Peter."

Bird forms   10.6.88

Incarnation in bodies other than human is not uncommon, and appears to depend on the life aspect the incarnating soul seeks to develop:~

"About birds and people inhabiting their bodies, Mary has said this is quite possible, and not so unusual either. Birds are quite high up in spiritual development in the animal races, and people feel more free if they come to Earth again through a bird, than in some human body. Intellectually, except for a few birds, they are a lot less advanced, but make up on the instinctual side. This doesn't matter to a soul who has just had an intellectual life, and wants a complete change.

Usually, the life in a bird's body is only quite short, but they become oriented on their mission, perhaps to help a relative, and as I say are free to fly the world in search of that relative. Anyway, that's what I have been told. But don't expect to see old uncle Arthur in the next cock-robin you meet though. It's not that common! Pete."

Summary   23.9.89

We incarnate to fulfil a life plan, from the difficulties encountered:~

"I have spoken in past chapters about one's need to fulfil a life plan, how difficult it is to complete the course you envisaged, and the amount of distress that is occasioned on returning here and seeing all too clearly why one was completely side-tracked by Earthly attractions. Some people may say,

'Oh yes! The work of the Devil'. I say to you now, the only devil you are radically over-estimating, is the one actually in your own personality. Here your hopes and fears reside to be influenced by all that makes up your material world. I want you to appreciate that it is you yourself who sanctions behaviour and response to any situation, not any demon outside.

I only want to stress that one's failures are not disastrous. One's ill gotten gains trouble you not, neither do they help you in any way once you are back here. But, that does not mean one's behaviour is of no consequence. The reverse applies, all we think and do remains part of our record in eternity.

Do not think 'left behind' is 'out of mind'. I assure you to ignore is your freewill choice, but can only result in stalemate, and any chess player knows that this is so aggravating to both players that it must be avoided if at all possible. The same principle applies here. But, unlike the chess player, the game is not lost. It does not have to be a fresh start. It can be linked more to a jigsaw puzzle. The pieces must be closely studied. If possible damaged pieces repaired, and if the final count shows some pieces to be completely missing, do not despair. Here there are experienced craftsmen quite accustomed to producing a substitute blank on which you are free to draw your own specification.

I must again emphasise, the choice is yours, and if life could only be lived once on Earth, there would not be re-evaluation of individual priorities. Some folk have the idea that a conscious effort to do good on Earth will assure them of immortality; a kindly pat on the head by God! I can assure you contact with God is tactically impossible for anyone of you who has not coped with all facets of your character. Like growing a number of precious plants on Earth, they must always be protected from the direct light emanating from God himself.

Each one of us must become gradually conscious of pure light. As our wicks are lengthened by experience, we can produce more light ourselves, and shall no longer be blinded by a brilliance at present beyond our very limited capacity.

Knowing that beauty exists, completes life's aspirations. Knowing, dictates our rising ambitions. I found on Earth, ambition was present in almost everyone in some degree. Surely, God would not want to give no scope for ambition and aspiration in his kingdom."

7. The Nature Kingdom

Dominion, Flowers and plant devas, Communing with plants,
Talking to the animals – Ants, Fish, Whales, and Cats,
Crystals and Devas, Devas – the builders of form.

Peter discusses our relationship to plants and animals and the spiritual nature of God's kingdom. All forms of life need to 'grow in spirit'; Man's awareness is his responsibility.

Dominion   Sept. '89

Talking to plants and animals is no longer so far-fetched. But the key is in 'thought', or telepathy, not speech, which bars our communication. In our ability to do so lies the potential for cooperation:~

"Our lesser brethren have humility of spirit compared to Man. If we add hardship to their path, we do ourselves an injury as well as them. Humility is the key to God's kingdom.

I came to the Spirit World a little unsure of relationships with the animal world. Actually, I had felt an affinity with all creatures on Earth. Bees I admired. They had seemed so independent and full of purpose. I could not understand people's fears of them, none stung me though I often picked them up. I tried to talk to them, and in my own imagination they responded. What must seem a childish dream is in fact reality.

The bar to communication is speech. We here do not use speech, concepts are entirely a thought process. Telepathy you are used to as a term. Question what you mean by this. Is it not a thought process, the manner of operation a closed book?

How can a transfer of ideas take place is something that tends to be a preoccupation of individual scientific studies. Mankind is unhappy unless the process is understood and can be repeated at will. Here we have no problem in repeating the process, and neither do we designate consciousness to the impractical process of belittling what we all know works!

Without speech, a discussion with animals is of no greater import than is discourse with a flower. Man himself expresses more opinion, and knows less of truth than our weaker brethren. What matters is that they know complete humility of spirit, which Man in his infinite wisdom has forgotten.

You see, Man's wisdom, as he would call it, is of his own making, not of God's. Our so called 'lesser brethren' do not have to struggle down the same road, but in due course will also find themselves in God's light. They will have followed a different path up the same hill. They, in the process, must interact with Man. Please remember that when you add hardships to their path, you do yourself an injury as well as them.

I hope, when first you are tempted to dismiss my words, you will give a little time to sitting quietly one early morning, and directing what you consider to be your Earth sensors towards a bright light which hopefully you will be able to see rising in the sky. It will of course be the Sun! No one around will be paying much attention to the phenomenon, even if they are enjoying the morning air. But, when you are fortunate enough to still share your surroundings with animals, you could well be amazed at their activities. I do not speak of domesticated creatures. Their natural instincts are destroyed in some measure by a behaviour pattern influenced by Man, but the wild creatures all recognise the omnipotence of the Sun. To them the day begins with acknowledging this; the birds sing, the ants start to rebuild their nests, the mice commence to stretch and clean their whiskers.

I know you will be saying, 'Ah, but many night creatures will not do so, they are sleeping.'

I say to you now, there is not one amongst them who will retire without cleaning its paws, remaking its bed, or verbally expressing its thanks to its creator for a day ending happily, secure once more for sleep, or expressing gratitude for another day in which to hunt or care for young. All wild creatures acknowledge Sunrise because they know upon the successful completion of this depends their very agreeable life style. By its very dependable routine, they are blessed with the privilege of life on Earth.

How often do Humans stop to acknowledge God's work, or to give thought to helping to fulfil a plan. Humility is the key which can open the door to God's love and eventually to his Kingdom."

Flowers and plant devas   22.5.88

The beauty of flowers in Summerland can be achieved on Earth when Man cooperates with the Devas:~

"Hello Dad. I have been visiting some of the public gardens in the city here. They are fantastic in their flowers in form colours and scents. If one is willing, and contacts the garden Deva, one can have a guided tour, being introduced to each group of flowers in turn, and being lifted into their world of energies; a world of colour, sound and love, beautiful and simple, yet beyond Earthly description.

I think, next time I incarnate, I will be a gardener, or botanist, and try to bring some of this beauty to Earth, if there is any place on Earth left unpolluted by man. I think I was a gardener in an earlier life a long time ago, but not very successfully! Perhaps, I can improve on that performance another time.

Please encourage (sister) Anne to go in for Herbalism. Perhaps, I can help her from this side. Plants have so much to give to help Man, if only they are allowed to grow naturally without artificial regimenting and forcing. This in itself encourages the spread of pests and disease, because the plants are weakened.

The Findhorn garden showed what could be achieved by natural means and co-operation with the Devas and plant spirits. But, of course, the gardening world on Earth scoffs at the idea of plant spirits, and *free* plant growth. It enslaves the plants, and forces chemicals on them in too great a quantity, which takes over the true plant life, weakens them and causes mortality. Much love – Pete."

Communing with plants   20.5.88

Devas are the guiding impulse of plant and tree growth. A telepathic rapport helps cooperation with plants, trees and all living creatures:~

"Good morning Dad!"

"It is a bright sunny morning here on Earth; a trifle nippy, but a good start to the day. Thinking about plants and the Findhorn garden yesterday, what communication do you have with plants, Peter?"

"Well, one can go to a plant, or a tree, concentrate one's mind on it, and be in telepathic rapport with it, as I am now with you. Plants live in a communal world of their own, and since they cannot directly move their roots to different places (unless they are Triffids!), they live much more as humans used to do before the advent of travel on Earth.

There are advantages in staying in one spot, one gets very deeply familiar with it, with the soil, the weather for that spot, and the characteristics of the Earth as a living being at that spot. Being part of a family, each plant partakes of the family characteristics, is not so individual as we are, and is in contact by telepathic means with its relatives in the family. The Deva for that group of plants is the overall guiding impulse for the growth and well-being of that plant, and as such is the entity to approach to get information on the species.

On Earth they are very wary of man, who does so much to damage the growth of plants, even when he means to do good. But here, man is full of care and concern for the plants and trees, and the Devas are quite happy to talk.

One has to remember that the plant world is on a different level to the animal world, and has its own ideals in life. What's best for a plant would not suit an animal! So, when one tries to communicate one has to accept this, and not force one's own irrelevant ideas on them, but try to understand their point of view. The requirements of a daisy are very different to those of an elephant! Providing one accepts this, one can have an interesting conversation with a plant Deva. They are quite intelligent, intuitive is perhaps a better word, in their own way. They can look into the future, so for hard times on Earth they try to make what provision they can for their species.

Here, of course, they do not have a physical body. So, what one sees is the astral body within which dwells part of the spirit of the species. Very beautiful! Must go now. Love from Peter."

Talking to the Animals – Ants   26.5.88

Peter's discourse with dolphins, whales, fish and insects—in their element—imparts a sense of the sacred nature of Life:~

"Morning Dad!"

"And to you Peter! What have you been doing?"

"Well, I have been talking to ants."

"How do you know which one to address, I thought they were all part of one entity?"

"Yes, they are so it doesn't matter which one you single out. They are all under the one Sub-Deva whose job it is to look after the nest. He reports to the Head Ant Deva, who in turn reports to the Area-Deva, who in turn reports to the Deva-in-Chief for all Ants. His address is Termite House, Anthill, Beds."

"I don't believe it Pete!"

"Well, something like that is true. They are very well organised, and in consequence can stand major losses like the destruction of an anthill without much trauma. Although, on the whole they don't like fighting humans, some species, like the red ants and the Soldier ants, don't hesitate to attack if humans stand in their way. They are really all on a war footing, and thus well equipped to survive.

I spoke to their Deva-in-chief (a very formidable figure from an earlier time), who had been removed to here by a steam roller. As you know, I don't like military things, but was forced to admire the ants' total organisation to carry on despite attacks on the Earth.

There is not too much love between ants. It is 'all for one, and one for all' sort of philosophy. Not really my 'cup of tea'."

Fish   3.6.88

"Good morning Peter."

"Morning Dad."

"It looks fine and bright here at present. What's the topic this morning?"

"Fish! Our rivers and streams and lakes are full of fish. The water seems living, bubbling, and singing, and one can talk to the fish as one talks to the animals, to get their point of view. One can dive into the water and move below it; there is no problem of lack of air, in fact one becomes charged up by the energy in the water.

When I did this recently, the fish all came round and were most interested in me. They had no fear, nobody catches them, and of course their world is quite different to the world we live in; water, plants and rocks, beautiful colours in the light pouring through it.

If one goes out into the oceans, so I am told, one can converse with the bigger fish, the whales and dolphins, and I hope to do that soon. They are particularly intelligent, and have their own ideas on how the world should be run.

The marine world is certainly quite different to our land world, but on Earth occupies much more of the Globe's surface. It is also getting very polluted by Man, and the fish have a lot to say about that! Love Peter."

Whales 7.6.88

"I joined a group of whales. Or at least I knew I was there. They didn't until I swam in front of their eyes. I had to be careful not to become a second Jonah, as they were busy sieving out Krill, as they went along with huge mouths open. They were enormous, but very gentle, and once they knew I was there started singing to me, and among themselves.

It took a little while to interpret the wonderful high and low singing notes, but the meaning eventually came through. They asked to be left in peace, and not hunted and killed. They said things had improved of recent years, but it still happened.

There were two or three babies among the group, and they kept close to their mothers, but were very interested in playing with me, which could be a bit alarming at times. I left the group with much regret, there was such a feeling of love and caring between them all. But, I promised to go back soon. Love Peter."

Cats 8.6.88

"Good morning Dad."

"Good morning Peter. Rather a wet one here."

"Beautifully fine this end! This morning I would like to talk about Cats."

"Well, we seem to have talked about mice, and snails and rats. So now it is cats!"

"They are usually quite psychic, and seem to have a good idea of what is going on in the higher planes. I have sometimes met them wandering in this area, and they often exchange a word if approached politely. They usually seem happy, but the hunting instinct is of course curbed. I think it is diverted into more intellectual pursuits, most seem quite knowledgeable.

Generally, they are on their own, though I understand there are areas devoted to all cats, where they live in mutual toleration. I told you I had met Rigel[1]. He seemed quite happy now, and sent his best purrs to Vega with love. Must go now Dad. Love to all – Peter."

---

1   Rigel and Vega are the Cowlins' pets.

6.1.89

"People try only to believe in their own omnipotence. It is a question of realising the truth of the matter which is that we all travel towards the same light. Some dogs come from higher spheres, also dolphins. You must understand that in those realms speech as we know it is not used. Must realise not a question of letters, only the thought that counts. Many cats are very intelligent in their understanding of things. Man thinks only he can understand!"

26.1.89

"I can speak to both physical and etheric animals. I like being with the physical animals because not many people try to hold a conversation with them."

"Is it a more equal situation on your side?"

"Yes. I know they (our cats) are sometimes annoyed that you restrict their movement. I mostly try to explain to them that it is the consequence of an experience they need."

11.4.89

Peter speaks of the large numbers of animals dying as a result of oil leaks:~

"I know that they experience nothing but joy once they reach here. They do not have the overlying problems that man has as the result of his knowledge which he has acquired, but misuses."

"No, I suppose they don't have regrets of actions done, or left undone that man suffers!"

"I enjoy my discussions with the whales and dolphins. They are so full of love and good feelings for the entire universe. They can pronounce sound dictates regarding important basic concepts of life. They are not overlaid by man's greed and self-interest."

Crystals and Devas   27.4.88

The inherent energy of crystals/stones is the domain of Devas. Peter discusses their work and their attitude to Man:~

"Please remember that stones, crystals, and all other forms that give out good energies, or bad energies, only have their own properties which they can use. Stones cannot put these things into themselves, they can only give out what is given them, but on their own vibration."

In referring to a particular piece of Fluorite crystal:~

"I should think it is unlikely that so much energy can get into many pieces of the Earth's fabric. I feel this is probably on account of its shape. I doubt many pieces come out of the Earth in such a form. The problem is a big piece assumes small proportions normally in handling because it is so soft. I feel that piece must have capabilities beyond most because it grew in that form, not having to be cut. It would need a very developed mind to transform a larger block to such a great power-house. I feel I have said enough on the subject."

"Could my 'bulk eraser' cleanse that crystal?"

"Yes."

"What about the warning in 'Cosmic Fire[1] *about the inimicability of crystal devas towards mankind?"*

"I hope my words are plain. No piece of the Earth's fabric can do damage on its own. The different elements have different vibrations, and the Devas are concerned with maintaining those vibrations, quite a job in itself.

Usually Mankind ignores the general principles of their construction, and uses them for his own gratification.

I am not advocating their general deployment without respect for their power. I can only say the Devas usually feel an ambivalence towards man, as he ignores their existence and efforts to maintain the status quo. I do not think they would engage in mischief if appreciated.

I feel they are present all around you, and do not trample on others who have a different role in God's plan. I feel that the Findhorn garden, which I know you are thinking about, was a very special big projection of energies for very specific reasons.

I do not want to suggest that you cannot make contact with a Deva. He will sense your love of his handiwork, and be inspired to work harder in your presence. But, I doubt you could hold a conversation. You might well be aware of his glow of pride if you are admiring his dedication – Pete."

1   *A Treatise on Cosmic Fire* by Alice A. Bailey

Devas, the builders of form   9.6.89

"Good morning Peter."

"Everyone has, ultimately, the same problems to overcome, but not everyone will be handling them in the same way."

"You are talking about broad characteristics, not everyone will turn out to be a pirate and a Judge. On starting everyone was the same, so why do differences become apparent?"

"Genes."

"How did genes become different?"

"Devas, the Elementals' work."

"As a potter makes different pots, so Devas make different bodies? God made Devas?"

"Yes everything."

"It is complicated for Man in a physical body. Is it plainer to you?"

"Yes, once one accepts Devas' work, it is easier to see some relevant dictates, and how life fits together. Try telling most people around you that they were constructed by Devas! See that you are out of reach!"

Summary

People's concern for natural wild animals does not extend to farm animals slaughtered for food. All animals share in their need for growth of spirit too:~

"Great store is set by being a happy and animal loving community. People are appalled at the realisation that only a few wild animals exist in their natural habitat, where only a short time ago herds could be seen by a limited number of tourists. Now masses of tourists search for animals. They too have the need to progress as spirits. They too do not die as believed by Mankind.

Strange that the concern for nature does not extend to those in our immediate environment. Perhaps you have never stopped to consider what happens to the Spirits of all the animals slaughtered for food. I can assure you they are all greeted in our world as is the human race, and quickly find joy and love amongst the beauty here.

However to raise their consciousness to a level from which they are able to face the brilliant light of their Creator, they too must refine their characteristics. No two have identical personalities, neither have they all coped in adversity to perfection. Can you give a thought to their needs, and in deciding your priorities, allow for helping their development.

Only sobriety can be experienced in total confinement. Little growth of Spirit can occur if they are fattened up for market, and are in other words treated as a convenient way of gorging our physical appetites. Do not think they do not care for confronting problems. Do not think they cannot understand your thoughts. They would not put your phrases on to paper, but they are as aware of the most basic of needs, as you are; namely they all seek loving relationships with those around, both human and animal, and vegetable. Just as they listen to your voice, so do they evaluate the vibration of the rest of Nature around them.

To them, all is sacred, and must be respected for its own role in the Cosmos."

8. Ecology and Environment

Man's interference, Damaging the Aura, Sea animals and pollution, Natural disasters, Re-evaluations.

The Earth may be made uninhabitable for Man, and all living creatures, if the present interference with natural balances for selfish aims is not halted. In this chapter, and in his summary, Peter discusses the challenge we face in the right use of Man's free will to determine the course of life on our planet.

Man's interference   19.12.87

The destruction of Man's environment would mean the loss of a testing area for mankind's evolutionary development:~

"Hello Pete!"

"Dad! This is one of the few areas, together with work in the Winterlands, where challenges do exist. The greatest ones are concerned with trying to steer the progress of Earth life away from its materialist course, (I remember still how difficult that used to be for me), into a more spiritual area, before destruction occurs to the whole physical side of the planetary life. The etheric planet would remain, but the physical might be made untenable as a testing place for man incarnate.

Some progress seems to have been made just recently in the arms agreement, but it is just a beginning, and there is a long way to go. Anything that can be done to raise the level of spirituality should be done by you on Earth, with our assistance and blessing.

Overhere the worry is that a first class testing area might not be available if all physical life is destroyed. There are other planets that could be used, but none that will support physical man's body as it stands at present. We would not worry too much if material living standards fell, though this would make return less comfortable for us, but it seems rather unnecessary if due to people's greed and short-sightedness.

Indeed, you see in the disaster areas of Africa somewhere that we can come to experience the test of hunger and deprivation, but like wars this involves a rapid turn round of souls, and a test of the willingness of the western nations to support their brothers in need. Not being met too well at present, I think! Must stop now – Pete."

9.2.88

"Morning Peter!"

"Dad!"

"Another very windy day is forecast. The weather seems to be changed, or changing from the usual winter pattern to a warmer, wetter, windier season."

"Yes, due to man's influence, the world ecosystem is being affected, and many up here are very worried that the balance will be so upset that physical man is wiped off the face of the Earth. Everything depends on everything else, and if the balance is too upset, what has been a temporary disturbance in the past will become a catastrophe.

Man's freewill enables him to alter the planet's surface irrevocably without actually realising what he is doing. Influences are being brought to bear on certain key individuals to warn of this, but it is not certain at present that this will be enough to stop the process. Man doesn't need to use the atomic weapons to ruin the Earth, it can happen from other causes insidiously. None of us here wish to reincarnate into such a mess, and the way it could go, life might not be possible. Not a cheerful prospect!

There are several ways life on Earth could go in the future, and the path depends on man's choice of what, at first sight, appear to be quite minor changes in lifestyle. Already, there is famine in Africa due to lack of rain, and too much rain in Europe, due to diversion of the weather pattern. Worse could come! I don't want to be a woeful prophet, but as many people as possible should know the options and consequences. Bye now – Pete."

12.4.88

"Morning Dad!"

"Well, what's the subject today?"

"The misuse of energies. The fact is that problems for Mankind can result from this cause. If the energies available to us were all used for the good of Mankind, and that includes the good of the Earth as Mankind's home, the world would be a happier, healthier place. Instead, Mankind uses energies available to it for selfish ends. The Earth is ravaged, and denuded of its mineral wealth, stripped naked of its trees and vegetation, its natural fauna reduced to a few specimens in a zoo, and He wonders why everything is in such a mess!

It seems that it is not until human beings arrive here that they are able to see what a state the Earth and Mankind is in. Or, if they do sense this while on Earth there is little they can do about it because they struggle against inertia, the lack of personal motivation and will, and the will of the selfish in power. Perhaps, if those that have the power to effect change realised they were going to have to return to live in all the mess they have helped to create, they would try to prevent the devastation that is taking place."

18.4.89

"A lot of people could regret the dredging of Earth's resources for selfish purposes. I am referring to mining, to oil, to forests, to the destruction of leylines, pollution of the atmosphere, the misuse of chemicals, the whole mismanagement of soil, the depletion of rivers and waterways, the excess eating, the knowledge of costly destruction of just about everything that has been freely given for the use of Mankind in the course of his learning. It is being destroyed solely for monetary gain, and for what is designated as 'comfort'.

Little is said by anyone in a position of authority about learning, except as an intellectual benefit. I feel only those interested in Nature, expect to gain useful knowledge to help other folk. It is an intensely distressing thing to actually watch the process on a grand scale, which in effect is what I can do from here."

"Must be, Peter. Painful!"

"Considering the behaviour of most Earth inhabitants, I cannot see any hope for the continuation of the species *in the same form.* I feel they may have to be faced with basic living problems again before a balance is restored.

Question is, how much of the vital elements will remain for the use of those of us who would wish to help with rebuilding a viable environment for Man to continue to practise control of his recalcitrant characteristics!"

"One needs basic things available to develop. Man has gone astray. He had a chance to rethink his values following the last major war, but developed the wrong things."

"I just hope continual backsliding can be halted. Do get the message across as soon as possible!"

"Today, I would like to talk about the state of the Earth's environment. The view from here is quite appalling, the more so for us who have to go back into what remains for other lives and make the best of it. Poisoning of the sea, the land, and the air and above, is taking place everywhere. Chemicals and radioactive compounds are released into the sea, which has a very limited capacity for absorbing them, unlike some people's imagination. The seas seem vast, but currents spread the noxious substances. Marine life has a low tolerance threshold for many of the poisonous substances, and following the death of plant life, and small creatures, comes the death of fishes, small and large.

On land, the surface of the earth is poisoned by chemicals, those put on to increase yield of food crops, denuding the soil without any replacement of natural humus. There is a start to natural farming methods, but it is minute compared to the world wide rape of the land by countries such as the U.S.A., Canada, U.S.S.R. and Europe.

Pesticides unbalance the natural flora and fauna, and pass into the food chain to affect you directly. Radioactivity released into the atmosphere gives fall-out which has affected hill farming areas in Cumbria and Wales due to their heavy rainfall. This has long-term implications.

Man's demand for energy has led to using up oil and coal supplies for little or no good return. Technical wonders like Concorde that use enormous amounts of fuel, are really an abomination of Ahriman.

Now you are finding problems with the distribution of energy by the grid wires that were unknown previously. The natural shield to the Earth, the ozone layer is being destroyed with disastrous results for mankind. The energy particles that were stopped by this layer, will now get through, and Man will be subject to much more ultraviolet radiation. As I said before, those about to incarnate into this mess, are horrified and fearful, though once they are down in a body again they will, no doubt, be drawn into the mass acceptance of the situation that seems to be the attitude of mankind.

Only a few brave and enlightened souls speak out against it all and try to initiate change – Peter."

6.6.89

"I note there is a growing concern on Earth now about climatic change. I feel I must point out that the change is inevitable. It is the degree to which you can determine the effective outcome by your control of Man's activities which is crucial. I suspect you will be in for a battle. I trust it will meet with a measure of success."

Damaging the Aura   15.5.88

The etheric field of the planet and of our own bodies is being interfered with. Such interference, which can give rise to disease, originates from stray electrical fields, contaminates in the atmosphere affecting the plant life and the food chain:~

"Morning Dad!"

"Good morning Pete! What's the subject today?"

"The human aura. You have been thinking of it, writing about it, lecturing on the subject, and using it to help people heal themselves for quite a while now Dad, and I think have come to the conclusion that it is electrical in nature. If it can be shown that disease can originate from its disturbance, the implications for the electrical supply industry are very far reaching!

The materialist society is built on foundations which include the extensive use of electricity in industry and the home. If it can be shown that some form of shielding is necessary round all electrical cables to prevent disastrous disturbance of our health, won't this be a considerable limitation, Dad?"

"It certainly will Peter. But, remember the strength of the stray magnetic field from an electrical cable depends on the strength of the current flowing through it. Again disturbance of the etheric field (which is probably the most likely one to be affected) might depend on frequency of the current. Also, we don't know how strong a field might cause disturbance."

20.10.88

"What's the subject this morning?"

"The life of plants today. Mum has been complaining about plants dying off, and not being able to start young ones as successfully as she used to do. All plants live on etheric energy, as we do—they all have their own auras—and when the flow of such energy is disturbed, plants suffer as much as we do.

There are so many contaminates in the atmosphere now from Man's industry that the flow of etheric energy has to pass through on its way down to us, that the quality and quantity of such energy available is poorer. Plants are very sensitive, and feel such change before we do. We shall also suffer from this change in the flow in time. When I say we, I mean incarnate Man. We in the Summerland won't be affected, except by the increased rate of souls returning to us. But, as I say, plants are more sensitive than Man or animals. They have to be, as they can't move position, and must record every little change in the atmosphere surrounding them.

People on Earth are presently worried about the breaks in the ozone layer, and the 'Greenhouse effect'. They should also be worrying about the change in etheric energy reaching them. But, of course, they mostly don't even know about etheric energy! Yet! Peter."

Sea Animals and Pollution   6.8.88

Peter relays the message of the seas:~

"I want to talk about the larger fish, and aquatic mammals. I went down to the oceans to meet them yesterday, and had to go quite a long way out to find them. They go in 'Schools', and I was able to talk to several of the dolphins as they rushed along together with a beautiful wave-like motion in and out of the surface water.

They said how much they liked the bubbly air mixture at the surface, and they were all very happy. The only thing they were worried about was the way some of the water was becoming a sort of chemical mixture, and they kept away from many river mouths, big ones especially, on that account. There was more fresh clean water in the deep ocean. They asked me to try to stop Man putting all his waste into the oceans and seas, because it is their home he is polluting. They have to live in it, and how would Man like it if his air was polluted! Which it is, at times, I pointed out. They thought it showed that man wasn't as intelligent as they had assumed!

I've been looking at the pollution in the North Sea, and it is really quite frightening. You might have thought it would be washed away by the surge of the Atlantic, but this doesn't seem to be the case. The prevailing westerly wind and currents tend to keep the waters trapped between Britain and the Continent, along with all the chemicals that pour into it from various sources such as the Rhine, the Humber, among many others. And now all the seals are perishing! The selfishness and lack of consideration of mankind for future generations, which means themselves, is quite frightening, and very saddening.

You and Mum have remarked on the lack of ladybirds to balance out the attacks of fly on plants. That is only one indication of the problem. Men think they can use their knowledge of chemicals to improve the balance of nature in their favour, but all they succeed in doing is to upset this balance which is very complex and very delicate.

Now they are destroying the natural ozone shield which protects them from the effects of UV radiation, and we over here can see a time when, from one cause or another, the world will become uninhabitable. This is why it is so essential for Man to realise his true constitution[1], and that the Earth life is only his school. The pupils are now rendering their school uninhabitable! They are blind to the consequences! Sorry to be so depressing, but thinking folk over here are very worried for the World. Love Peter."

11.8.88

"This reccurring disease of the seals in the North Sea seems tragic Pete."

"It's another consequence of Mankind's abuse of nature. He pours chemicals and noxious substances over the land, into the rivers, and finally into the sea, and expects life to carry on as though such pollution didn't exist! It's been going on for years, steadily getting worse, and the chemical manufacturers with the blessing of the government, reap big profits, and have little interest in the final resting place of their products.

The few people who have had the imagination to see the catastrophic outcome of this deadly trade, have been shouted down by those interested in lining their pockets. They have the backing of a government less interested in preserving the balance of nature, than preserving the balance of trade! In consequence, it is only when tragedies such as the death of all seal life in the North Sea have occurred that any number of people are aware that this state of pollution really exists.

My seal friends were very worried about the situation, and rightly so! Their opinion of mankind was very low indeed. 'Lack of intelligence', and 'no thought for other life', were their comments! Must go now – Peter."

---

1   The constitution of Man is discussed in Chapter 5 under *'Soul and personality'*.

Natural Disasters   1.9.88

Peter discusses disasters such as drought, and excessive rainfall caused not only by Man's handiwork, but also by the Earth changes. The Earth is going through a change which in itself, may lead to natural chaos:~

"Very wet this morning here. A good start towards Autumn. We don't seem to have had much summer this year, only a few weeks of sunshine."

"The change in weather patterns may be bound up with Man's pollution of the atmosphere. In which case Mankind can only blame itself for the natural disasters such as are occurring now: drought leading to famine, and excessive rainfall leading to flooding. If our world civilization continues on the course it is set on, it looks from here as though the Earth will be soon uninhabitable. We shall either die from our own pollution, or be killed off by natural disasters originating from the disturbance to the balance of nature. Man unguided by his Soul, has not the wit or wisdom to run the earth safely while he indulges in this materialism. What a pity, it's all rather unnecessary! Peter."

12.9.88

"What's to talk about this morning?"

"Natural phenomena of the world. Recently, we have seen in Bangladesh, the Sudan, and Ethiopia, natural disasters due to flood, drought, and famine, and the massive loss of life that follows. These have been mainly in the third world countries, but such disasters on a similar scale could occur in Western countries. Indeed, we have had hurricanes in Europe which did so much damage to Britain's trees in the South.

It is not so many years since the massive flooding in East Anglia, and London. Flood walls, and barriers have been erected since then, but it only needs an extra rise in level of the North sea, to overtop these and repeat the disaster. Man's treatment of his environment can more easily than generally appreciated lead to these sorts of disasters, and the body of the Earth needs to be treated with much more care and respect than is usual if disasters are to be avoided in future – Peter."

18.10.88

"What have you been doing recently Pete?"

"I have been to talks about Geophysics."

"What have you gathered from those?"

"The Earth is in one of its regular phases of changing it's size, and angle of rotation, which is likely to cause chaos everywhere as it happens.

Changes of size will cause more earthquakes, and volcanoes to appear. Changes of angle of rotation will cause tidal waves if it happens quickly, and flooding if it happens slowly."

"Is this all additional to the build up of carbon dioxide, the 'Greenhouse' effect?"

"Yes, one can expect large scale happenings from now on for a while. Their severity is partially dependent on the rate at which they happen."

"What fun!"

Re-evaluations

14.2.89

World events and personal experiences are stronger and more rapid due to the incoming new Age. A happier world is possible, but *helpful* actions are needed:~

"A lot of trouble is around in the world at the moment."

"Yes, Peter. The news shows one problem after another."

"Question of not realising *why* they are occurring."

"I accept they are experience, but most people won't think of them in that light."

"I told you that the reason for such experience, at the present time, is great because of the coming Age. Much has to be sorted out. God's plan must become successful eventually, and if things fail to move forward, a desperate effort has to be made to help. Hence a rapid breakdown of so much is going on, but hopefully good is to emerge from what you describe as chaos.

I know that, to you, a collapse of so much that appeared stable is traumatic, but everyone has a part to play, and when values are reassessed a happier world becomes possible. The bottom of the pot is yet to come, and those who cannot rise above material needs will suffer most."

"When you say, 'rise above material needs', on Earth one has basic needs, food, shelter, and love, which are missing in many countries."

"Yes I see what you mean. A lot of this might be alleviated if Man could dedicate more effort to helping his brothers rather than fighting."

"Fighting for power heads the list of the causes behind a variety of the major problems."

"It applies in different forms. Unfortunately it has become very much a stumbling block for you in desperate moments. The justice of action is forgotten, and power is used to try to make the situation better. Calm evaluation of all that is involved appears not always to get a look in. Sufficient background is not considered because that implies re-evaluation of past standards of behaviour. I know you have to live in the world as it is. But wisdom should enable you to see what you can usefully do to effect change for the good."

"Don't let all our feathers get ruffled continuously, you are saying? I will try to remember that when looking at the news."

"A lot is bound to disturb you, but you gain nothing by discussing, unless you can take some action after you have reached a conclusion. All else is energy expended to no purpose."

"There must surely be a good reason for discussing with people to a minimum degree. Unless there is such discussion different votes may not occur in another election. Also, a change in eating habits and the nuclear programme for example, are less likely to occur without discussion."

"Yes, I did not mean no discussion. I meant it was useless unless its aim is an assessment for action of some sort, no matter how small a step it may seem. Bye for now."

Summary

Man lacks the concept of 'togetherness'. He fails to see the unity of the cosmos—the interrelatedness of all things—and this leads to misuse of Earth's resources:~

"A special link with both Ecology and Environment is dependent on one's conception of the world. I want to point out that a misunderstanding concerning the unity and interrelatedness of physical life bedevils Mankind's attempts to influence the development of each in harmonious growth for the well-being of his own and future generations.

I realise Man lacks the concept of togetherness. He believes plants, animals, minerals, not to mention the stars, the weather, and the life-

-giving force of energetic homogeneous entities, have no part to play in the way life is organised. He sees them as God's creation, but not as a living part of the cosmos which he shares, rather than owns, for development. He needs to work with them all.

The knowledge of eternity should enable a different perception. Like a human being, the other constituents of the Universe have a response to abuse too. They wither and die if love is denied them, and if the necessary conditions for growth are not met, they do not continue to exist in a form that can be utilised on earth. Sadly the current result of misuse is now apparent. Man must help regerminate and revitalise Earth's resources for the future well-being of other Souls."

ECOLOGY AND ENVIRONMENT

Part 2

Reviewing Past Lives—
Learning by Experience.

Introduction to Part 2

A summary of purpose, Introduction.

Part 2 concerns the purpose of life. In *Records of Past Lives*, Peter outlines the evolutionary growth of Spirit and goes on to describe events and lessons gleaned from recalling his own previous experiences on the physical plane. The process by which we may ourselves come to assess our own life experience is revealed in the example of Peter's review of his past lifes.

In the review of his most recent life as Peter, he suggests that when one has resolved certain facets of behaviour over a series of lives, the need to re-experience them is over, and the next step upon the evolutionary path can be taken.

In *Communications from Other Folk*, a similar theme presents itself: that we gain from understanding experience. These communications reveal how people felt on arriving in Summerland and how they are often little changed in character unless motivated by personal effort. This chapter illustrates the variety and complexity of human experience, and the progress individuals are making toward their understanding.

The struggle to master our failings and the ability to contain our behaviour toward the development of spirit is presented in the final chapter, *Reason For Life on Earth*.

The summaries provided at the end of lives 1 and 2 reveal how patterns of behaviour are resolved through the lessons of a particular life experience, how the character or personality we choose is designed to present optimum opportunity for such experience, and how the guidance throughout life ultimately comes from the soul.

A summary of purpose   18.6.89

The Akashic record is an imprint on the Spiritual world of all that
has ever happened; from them one must try to unravel one's
successes, failures, and one's future needs. The purpose of recall
and the linking of details from the Akashic records, requiring
considerable determination, is summarised by Peter:~

"The essential material that follows is my thought on how different
lives helped my development in Spiritual expansion."

1.9.89

"Let me summarise the purpose. I have the feeling that this
description of existence, and its purpose, will surprise many readers,
and be totally abhorrent to some who hold an impeccable picture of
Heaven, and of God. I know for these readers my story will remain
a fiction. Perhaps, for just a few I shall have opened another door.
I desire to do just that, because we all must make our own way up the
mountain.

For us all there is only one Creator whom we call God in the
Western world. I would suggest that in all religions Man is looking
for hope, and seeking love and support in the troubles he faces in
life. This is common ground for all of us. Please let your hearts open
to what is kind and good, not to dissension and turmoil.

Readers should approach these words in humility of self, and of
such openness of heart, that they have time to wonder rather than
dismiss out of hand.

I know that upon Man's ability to love and to wonder, depends the
future hopes and fears of Mankind. God made the world, and a mass
of His work is still not as yet appreciated. It is a question of
awakening the consciousness that is the key to knowledge.

I assume goodwill in Man's heart in trying to bring together
evidence of the survival of Death."

Introduction — by June Cowlin

By Christmas 1987 there had already been many communications
from Peter; there was no doubt about a continued existence. I
recalled my words at the hospital,

"Oh Pete, I'm going to miss you so much, please communicate if
you can!" He had done so, offering all the assurance he could that

there is survival of death, and yet an enormous hole remained in one's life, all the messages were dependent on a third person.

"If only I could speak with Pete," I thought, "I might tolerate his physical absence."

New Year's Eve only served to emphasise the inevitability of accepting the situation; it could not be changed.

"Why not try using the pendulum", Michael suggested. I was aware of the possibility of making contact with "the other side" by this means. Now, I had an incentive to approach this with due reverence, and not to dismiss what might initially appear a response of little consequence without giving it a fair trial. Slow beginnings led to an agreement to sit quietly at a specific time prepared to converse. Initially, it was a painstaking effort for both sides, and the exchange with communicators was brief. But, telepathic rapport gradually improved, and speed and complexity of communication increased with confidence and an assured acceptance of what one was personally experiencing.

Apart from Peter, the channel was also used by others, including relatives giving their personal viewpoints.

In a script recorded on the 28th November 1987, Peter began to indicate his attention being drawn to reviewing his past lives when speaking of people he had met who had known one another before, and who had memories of earlier lives:

"Mine don't seem to have come back much yet. Perhaps I ought to have a think about them, though I've been told not to worry, as they would appear soon enough."

And on 8.12.87:

"I keep bumping into people that I have known before!"

"In this life?"

"No, mostly in past lives. They seem vaguely familiar at first, then a sort of remembering comes back."

"How much do you remember of past lives?"

"Not very much at present, except where I had contact with these people, then something comes back, like a dream you sort of remember partially. Sometimes part of it returns in a rush. I seem to have been associated with big houses, I suppose that's why I like big rooms, but just how isn't clear to me yet. I'm told it is early to remember a lot about past lives. This will all be made plain, together with how I did in them, later."

On the 12th January 1988 my own Mother (who died in 1985) spoke of various family members, and then said: "Peter has links, related before in earlier lives." Speaking with her at the end of January I questioned whether she could put names to photographs in an old Victorian album. She had not been able to do so in life. She did not respond to the suggestion, but at the beginning of February 1988 Peter drew attention to this album, claiming it had once belonged to him, as Charles Pizzey. This was to be the start of a discourse lasting many weeks during which Peter identified a number of people represented in the album, and brought some of them to the channel to give their own information about their last life on Earth.

How much of this information was already known? None beyond my own mother's generation. The album had belonged to my grandmother, who died in 1933. Suddenly, information previously thought of vague interest assumed vital importance. So much family history had been given, there must be a purpose. Was the family review an effort to support the quite widely held proposition that we have serial lives?

We knew we must try to substantiate some of the details which would support Peter's claim that he had been my grandfather, who died as a young man. (Peter is our son by adoption.)

We bought books on Genealogy which clearly warned us of the pitfalls: clandestine marriages, particularly before Hardwicks Act of 1754, no penalties for failing to register a birth before 1875, errors in entries and different spellings of names; different names used in daily living from that officially given (we realised that to be true amongst our own circle of friends). Also, the warning; 'Do be prepared to accept the occasional indiscretion in every family'; that applied to those in possession of some useful leads, old letters, older members of family who might recall a valuable snippet of family history. My relevant family were all "in the beyond", no marriage or death certificates had survived to give a lead.

My information was from a discarnate source, and much of personal interest was related. Details of Peter's past life, and those of other members of the family, are presented. A lot of research remains to be tackled.

9. A Record of Past Lives

Parts of one whole, Past lives identified, Rich Life, Overseer, The Gardener, The Smuggler, The Judge, Memstec, Charles Pizzey, Peter.

In this chapter Peter reviews past reincarnations up to the recent one, which he covers in more detail. The review of one's most recent life is experienced by everyone.

Peter outlines the concept of the evolutionary process of Spirit in *Parts of one whole*. He goes on to discuss, in reviewing previous lives, the character traits needed to be altered, and the opportunities for handling them that were often wasted.

One makes a life plan before each reincarnation. Some characteristics recur sequentially, others may have been successfully handled, or may not be required in the plan for the further incarnation. One is enabled to grow spiritually through effort.

Peter completes his life reviews in *Summary of life as Charles Pizzey*, and at the end of this chapter.

Parts of one whole   17.5.91

"Understanding the importance of Spirit is essential to comprehending eternal life. It is the permanent portion of Mankind. Aeons of time ago it broke away from God. The subtle emanation must be calibrated both in density and fluidity in order to return. I know this is developing an Earthly concept, but do not think it is one with which scientific man can take exception.

It is in order to achieve this transformation that Mankind incarnates. Delineation on Earth is through emotional and physical experiences. Hence, we must have a variety of opportunities. Because we are eventually able to control the character of these experiences, as well as the way a response is made, *we do not always need all the properties of all the energies*. At subsequent incarnations we can ultimately manage with less. To put it another way, we have coped!

The question will arise of eventually reuniting the whole. This is always done in the Spirit body which is totally conscious of the state of man's value all of the time, hoping to construct a permanent, spiritually whole being, that is once again in full unison with God.

We therefore bring to each incarnation the portion of spirit that still needs to achieve perfection. The total Man exists all the time, but the portion on Earth constitutes the mass in early stages of experience. Later, deliberate decision will be made to leave some component behind. If you consider the Earthly equivalent of fashioning an enormous panoramic composition, we do not need all of the tools all of the time. We eventually perfect a portion, and then the whole.

In the case of Mankind, for all but a few, work must take many more centuries. This is a deep concept, I hope some insight can be gained."

Past lives identified

Peter gave information concerning earlier lives, as set out sequentially below:~

1) Peter Cowlin, 1969 to 1987. Still a student at time of accident.
2) Charles Pizzey, 1860 to 1899. Lived in London. In Service from age 13 years. Trained as a Butler. Was a Manager of a Public House when he died suddenly, leaving a wife and three children.
3) A Negro Man named Memstec, 1796 to early 1832. Died from injury in an attack. Had engraved pistols made by his father until the business was closed down by white authorities. Became a jobbing gardener/handyman to the rich household in which his mother was employed.
4) A Judge in 1600's in Austria. Studied in Vienna, worked in Lienz/Villach district. Had a sizeable family. Was well thought of by the authorities, but harsh on 'the criminals', and hard on his family.
5) Organiser of Smugglers in 1500's in Polperro. Was happily married, and had a fairly long life. Had to 'stay on top', if necessary, by force.
6) A Gardener in Devon (circa 1406) to a rich family named Boniface. In love with the daughter of the house.
7) A Roman Soldier.
8) An Overseer, again in Roman times. Oversaw the building of an Arena, not in Rome itself.
9) Court Jester, in Crete.
10) A previous life recalled as a rich person.

Peter summarises the opportunities taken and lessons gained in his most recent lives at the end of the appropriate sections.

The sequence of lives is given in reverse order, i.e. from first to last. The earlier lives contain the underpinning lessons that form the basis of subsequent experience.

A rich life   Life no.10

The following is based on information given between February '88 and June '89:~

"I have spent quite a lot of time endeavouring to understand why a difficult rich life presented few opportunities for progress. I seem to have had little incentive to become more understanding of others."

"Do you think that was your intention?"

"Yes, possibly it was to connect wealth with understanding the lot of others."

"Would not these concepts be conveyed by wiser folk on your side?"

"No. People need to work them out for themselves. I told you about discussion classes. The question is what you make of the talks."

"Seems to me to be an extremely drawn out business. Hate to think how many lives are needed to get anywhere!"

"Yes, many. Death is only a stepping stone. It's a question of total commitment to service here, too."

The Overseer   Life no.8

17.6.89

"I did not think you could be clad in so many shades of knowledge. I find I have had a life in the past which involved controlling the building of a complete arena for Roman games.

I used to control the arrival of stone. So much material was used, and so many people engaged in the process, that several men had to be responsible for how the material was dealt with when it reached the site, otherwise chaos would have caused fighting amongst rival groups.

The behaviour of a lot of them was not very disciplined. The discipline was enforced by destroying confidence in themselves, and creating large numbers of obedient robots. Even in the army of those days, there was no room for individual character. Individual thought was not encouraged.

This was not a life of glory. It was bedevilled with problems, which could only be solved by force of strength. In the position I held I had the power to enforce conduct considered necessary, and direct work efficiently. It involved much brutality and fear.

I did not belong to the elite of those times. I was secure as long as things went well, so my own life depended on no insurgence within the lower ranks."

"Do you know which arena you were involved in?"

"No, I do not think it was Rome itself that I lived in."

"Any idea how long these arenas took to build?"

"I could not put it accurately in terms of earth years, but it was not completed in a day."

"Did you see it completed?"

"Yes, but I did not work there all my life. Coagulation of the project was my dambusting effort. The pressure was greatest as the time of completion drew nearer. Nerves were frayed, and everybody thought, because heaving massive building material involved only strength, progress should go like a pendulum. Many died in the process. I lasted forty-five years which was good going in perfect condition."

"You don't know which emperor was around?"

"No, I guess they came and went fairly quickly in many instances. One had no time to involve oneself with politics. If one was an instrument of importance for providing a good life for the nobility, one stuck to the priorities in order to survive. I had a wife and children, and a home. I was therefore in a good position, blissful in fact, for my lowly rating in the hierarchy of the times.

I learned that hard work could influence a life, and realised that in a lowly position it sometimes made the difference between life and death. I know now that this should not necessarily be so. The question is not completely geared to fairness, only to everyone being submissive, and collapsing on the job. There were no state benefits to ease the individual suffering, really a case of sink or swim!"

"I suppose so, though were there not the temples and holy people who tried to help?"

"Not the ordinary people, only those tarred with the brush of influence. Their numbers affected life's outcome. It was not possible to give attention to the copious osmosis of humanity."

"Interesting, are you still going back in lives?"

"Yes, I give some time to the consideration of earlier experiences. It's a question of knowing how one's understanding of situations came about.

I am beginning to find we are closely linked in many lives. I am not sure in what way yet."

The gardener

"I once lived at a big house down in Devon."

"In one of your past lives?"

"Yes."

"Which part of Devon?"

"I think north Devon."

"We stayed in that area, Combe Martin."

"Lots of hassle."

"In that house?"

"Yes."

"Affecting you?"

"Yes. I loved the daughter of the house."

"What position were you in at the time?"

"I was helping in the garden."

"So you loved above your station? Hence the hassle! What period of time was this?"

"1406."

"Early part of the fifteenth century. Any idea of a name of house or village?"

"Only know it belonged to a family named Boniface."

"That's interesting. Any idea what the man did? Was he a fighting man?"

"I think he travelled buying lots of expensive scent."

"The aromas of the east! Did he have French connections?"

"He was away a lot, hence the gardener played with the daughter."

"What happened?"

"I got a lot of comfort from knowing she would have liked to run away."

"With you? Eventually did you get sacked?"

"Yes. I am not sure of all the details yet."

The smuggler

"Do you have a road map to look at. Try to find southern England, Devon. I want to show you where I lived in an earlier life. (Indicated Looe area). Not Looe, Polperro."

"Were you a fisherman?"

"Yes, I used to travel to other customs officers."

"You were something to do with control of goods coming into the port?"

"I controlled smuggling gangs."

"What used to be smuggled?"

"Spirits from France, brought ashore at Polperro. I once had a meal in an old house which was familiar to me. I realised I had known the place before when I reached the congested street going down to the duty quay."

(Peter had once camped in Cornwall)

"When would that be?"

"1589. I made money illegally by bringing drugs into England from regular trips to the East. I had a reasonably happy home life and lived to tell many a tale."

24.10.88

"I was not a smuggler myself except at the start. I controlled gangs of smugglers and took the profits."

"A sort of mafia godfather?"

"Yes, you could call it that!"

"Who did you sell the drugs to that you brought into the country?"

"The quantity was quite small by present day standards, and I sold to members of the aristocracy who were committed to taking drugs at that time. I got a good profit on such sales."

23.1.89

"I told you about my reincarnation a long time ago, when I was in Cornwall."

"Ah, yes, as a manager of smugglers at Polperro!"

"I see that I tried then to give fair reward to those who smuggled for me. I found that the value of giving good wages was that they remained loyal, but once they felt hard done by, they were likely to ricochet. I tried to be reasonable with them, but eventually, the question of my own safety arose. Hence I learnt to have no mercy on defaulters."

"Thus it is still said even these days, such people seem only to understand dire handling. They abuse one's generosity of spirit."

"I realised some used to take drugs themselves, and therefore became quite dangerous. Control did not exist."

"You mean help in any form? You were engaged in illegal operations anyway."

"I had to handle it myself. This meant killing to stay alive. This I loathed. I needed help so I took to heavy drink."

"Was that the start of a drinking problem?"

"No, drink was a difficulty in an earlier life."

"It has been for you in various forms throughout the ages. You had to be tough with your staff."

"I henceforth decided to get my own back on such people, not by trying to reform them, as is the accredited way in social work circles now, but by taking the law into my own hands."

"Being Pete, there were no half-measures. Having made up your mind you did a good job! I can understand your reaction!"

"From this life you can gather how I decided to go into law. I studied relentlessly next time round. I then made the mistake of believing power was the answer.

"There are plenty these days who believe that the answer is to squash the problem! In the times you are talking about, the response was even more drastic."

"The outcome was that this time I gave the orders, others did my bidding."

"Because you didn't have to grapple with them personally. So this was your effort to understand law and order."

The judge   Life no.4
                                               5.6.88

"I must tell you about my life in Austria. I lived in 1672 and worked as a judge. In time I will know more, but I have got recollections that I tried criminals. I used to be mostly concerned with fraud. Life was more crude then.

I feel, because I often was hard on these folk, I had to experience the other side of life. I know I will have to be more efficacious in handling people in future."

6.6.88

"I would like to talk about my past life in Austria. I told you that I was a judge. I lived in Lienz, a town in the south. I also sometimes visited Wien in the summertime when travel was easier. There were big mountains between the area and the northern part of Austria, and roads were blocked in winter.

Times were hard, and so was I! One had to keep the peace, so anyone that transgressed I put in prison, or had whipped, or hung. We didn't spend too long in deciding they were guilty. If it seemed to me that there was a probability of them being guilty, I dealt with them anyway. That alone provided a deterrent for others! There were wars, and other disturbances and we wanted peace and order. That was my job and I was good at it. I criticised everyone, and dealt swiftly with anyone who came to my court. That was what I was paid by the government to do. I saw nothing wrong in that at the time."

"Did you marry and have a family?"

"Yes, I had a good Austrian wife, who looked after my house and bore me children."

"How many?"

"I think there were six, but some died early. I had order in the family too. I was a judge and head of the family, so everyone had to respect me, or else! My wife was the only one who dared say a word to me, and that not often. When I was annoyed, they all shook in their shoes.

We lived in what was a big chalet-type house in the centre of Lienz, and had a number of servants to run it, which they did like clockwork, or paid the penalty! My word, I was efficient! So were they, or they didn't last long!"

30.6.88

Commenting on someone he believes to have been linked to him in the Austrian life:~

"Most judges have lots of acquaintances, not many friends!"

17.7.88

"I told you about recalling my life as a judge. I used to say to criminals that they would go to hell, heaven was only for good people."

"Now you know differently!"

"Know that people make their own hell. Everyone has experienced bad times, and come to terms with them. Don't conclude that because people do dreadful things they must be half-witted. Many are a great deal more advanced than most of us."

30.8.88

"I have looked at my life as a judge again. I was trained in west Vienna."

"A law school?"

127

"I studied very hard, but I don't think I referred very often to the law."

"You meted out rough justice! You knew what was laid down, but did not take it too seriously."

"I got people beheaded for stealing! I found I totally abused my power."

"Does this mean you will have to come down again to try handling power better?"

"I find this frequently is a learning situation for me. Both of my recent lives were the outcome of that misuse of power. I tried to make amends this time round by helping some of those I had misused."

"Are you saying that some of the people you came in contact with in your last life were under your legal eye in the 1600's?"

"Yes. I want everyone to know that I tried to be just in this last life. I thought by doing someone a good turn I would relieve my guilt."

"Well your personality didn't realise that this time round, did it?"

"No."

"But your higher self felt this. Your friends said you were always helping someone. So your higher self had seen the mistake, and was trying to right the balance."

20.1.89

"I find I misused my progress in deciding to be important, back in 1680. I had grasped a lot of bonafide ideas in earlier lives, but I thought this made me an important person. I misused my feeling of superiority by haranguing dossers."

"You mean people who do no useful work, layabouts, those that got into mischief and got caught!"

"My belief then was that they were a bad lot."

"Still a widely held feeling today amongst those who have not developed much inner knowledge."

"I suppose it's mostly to do with a lack of appreciation of knowing that we are all on a similar road, but there are different paths leading off to the top. I like to think I could handle ripe potential now more adroitly. I now realise there is purpose in our earth lives in a way I did not before."

"What about your return to your present side after these other lives? What happened then?"

"I find I continued to lie around. Like so many I did not see the way ahead."

"But, before your life in 1680 you had some insight. So, when you returned to the other side, was it with much clearer insight then?"

"No, I quickly lost what I had briefly seen!"

"This concerns me. How often does one do just that rather than keeping the acquired insight?"

"I think people need to experience many aspects of problems before moving on permanently in terms of understanding."

"The same problem handled with different abilities from a different angle. A colossal task."

"Knowledge is hard experience. Not learned from books. Everything you do for yourself is experience, while things others do for you gives much more limited knowledge of the subject."

"It has it's part presumably?"

"Yes, accepting help is again an experience we must have, otherwise we would not suspect we had any weaknesses."

"Do you want to say any more about the 1680 life? There must be positive things from it!"

"Not necessarily. Not all lives have a great deal of progress associated with them."

"If they were all highly progressive, we would not need so many lives, or need to re-experience things."

27.1.89

"In my life as a judge I feel perhaps I managed to give time to mystical things. You see I had considerable understanding by then of these matters. That is why it was my aim to use this knowledge whilst in a position of influence. A great deal depended on the response of others, and you know a lot of tolerance is needed there."

"Yes Pete, you are quite right!"

"I realised many of my confederates did not have my spiritual understanding, and most of those I sentenced were unable to appreciate the finer things of life because all their energies were released on dealing with physical survival."

"Yes, none too much time to think about anything else!"

"I just lacked sufficient maturity of a directional nature to handle the position I held. Only wanted to survive my stint without losing the respect of those that mattered in the end."

"Your higher standards went by the board."

"I now realise that I bit off more than I could chew! I feel I have a bone I may have more opportunity to grapple with in the future."

"It's a big bone!"

"I know I may be unable still to achieve perfection, but I hope I can do better than last time."

"I imagine to achieve perfection is asking too much. As you pointed out, one has to have several lives before achieving what is desired. So, are you saying a positive aspect of the life was the time you gave to mystical considerations?"

"Yes."

"That hopefully did something for you. Anything else about that life?"

"I was not a very charitable person."

"Your mystical thoughts did not help in your tolerance or understanding of others?"

"No they just added to my feelings of superiority."

"Another big danger, 'holier than thou'. A pitfall to be guarded against."

Memstec

Life No.3

8.3.88

"I'm about to start looking at the life before the one as Charles Pizzey. I think we were close in that life."

"Where did it take place Pete?"

"Washington, in America."

"Any idea of the year of birth or death, Pete?"

"Born 1796, died 1832."

"So you lived for 36 years, about the same as life no2. Anything else about that life you can tell us?"

"Yes, I was black! I'm going into this one fairly slowly, Dad. It's got some rather unpleasant features, and the memory is a bit painful. I know I died from being hit on the head with a stick, and that memory is not pleasant to go back to... "

13.3.88

"I am still reviewing life no.3 as a child."

"Any more revelations?"

"Yes, some of them concern you and mum. I grew up as a black child in a white family in Washington. My parents were servants in the family, and the family was comparatively enlightened and good

130

to us in their own way. However, the climate was one of oppression of the black population, and it was a difficult life.

Can you imagine what it is like to be regarded as the lowest of the low, and treated like dirt by all but a very few, who themselves ran a risk of being censured if they appeared too friendly? Not pleasant! So I don't wish to dwell on that life too long. I really want to see how the connecting thread ran and how I performed, what led me to life no.2, and then life no.1."

18.3.88

Peter also mentioned that his mother had been a servant who made rugs in her spare time and that his father made pistols which he himself engraved. After the father's death, he and his mother 'lived in' the big house where she worked and that he had set fire to his room when roasting pigeon. He had one sister, Rebecca:~

"You were saying last night Pete that your dad in life no.3 was a maker of pistols. How does that square with your description of your parents as servants in a white family?"

"Well my mother was a servant throughout my life. My dad started as a servant, a helper to a pistol maker who died leaving my dad knowledgeable about the trade. So, he carried on his own. Hence we had our own house. That's how I am picking it up now anyway. A sort of far memory of events. At that time pistols were much in demand. There was a lot of violence about and people needed a pistol for personal protection."

"You said your mother then made rugs. How did she make them when she was a servant?"

"She made them after her day's work, for extra income. Her employer was quite enlightened and allowed her time to do this. But, the feeling against us in the white community was quite strong. They didn't like coloured people getting much money. I suppose they thought it threatened them. In the southern states of course, conditions were terrible for coloured people. They were nearly all slaves. So we were luckier than most."

22.3.88

"... about life no.3, it seems after I set fire to my room roasting pigeon that I got a reputation as a fire raiser quite undeservedly. Though I was fascinated by watching fire, I did not start any deliberately but was accused of doing so whenever there was a fire in the district. Luckily the charge was not provable, though being black was a definite disadvantage. I thought it very unfair."

131

"Can you say any more about how your dad made those pistols?"

"Well, all the parts were bought in; barrel, lock, etc. We made the wooden handle or stock, and put the bits together. Then we chased an ornamental design on the metal, polished the wood, and dad put the name of the firm on it. I used to help with the engraving and got quite good at it."

31.3.88

"For a while I helped my dad in the gun-making business, and trade went well. Then one day soldiers came into the shop and said they were taking it over, and that it wasn't right for a black man to run a business. It was most unpleasant. Dad and I were turned out of the business, we had to find what we could in the way of employment doing odd jobs. I worked as a gardener for a while, and as a houseboy to rich families in Washington.

My mother continued as a servant with the same rich family she had been with. Somehow we kept our house going. It was only a small one but it was home. I was eighteen then, and dad was about forty."

12.4.88

Peter identifies the rich lady in whose household his mother worked as Harriet, being also his mother June in his most recent life:~

"I know I pinched lots of money that mother made me pay back. The rich lady I think was you June."

13.4.88

"That was most interesting to learn that your mum here was the rich lady for whom you worked then. Any more items of interest?"

"Well, I mentioned that we lost the gun-making business, turned out because we were 'niggers', and that we worked at various odd jobs. Eventually, my dad died of a fever, and left mum and myself to struggle as best as we could.

Luckily the rich lady my mum worked for continued to employ us. I worked in her garden, though her husband did not like me at all. I suppose I wasn't servile, not enough for him anyway, but she stood up for me and my mum, so we stayed on.

This went on for some years, until one day I was out on an errand; I can see it now like a play. A crowd had gathered around someone who had been hurt, a white man.

Someone in the crowd shouted, 'That's him!' pointing at me, and then they all turned and started to chase me. I ran away and would

132

have outdistanced them, but I caught my foot in something and fell. The next moment I felt a blow on my head and went unconscious.

Looking at the drama from outside my body as it were, it was a big man with a black beard that hit me with a stick, on the head. The crowd grabbed me and took me to the local gaol, where I was thrown on the floor of a cell. Eventually, I woke up with a terrible headache, and blurred eyesight. Someone looked through the bars and said,

'No, that's not the boy.' Then the officer made me get up and threw me out on the street again. I just had to crawl back to the house, and was put to bed. The rest is very hazy, but a few days later I came back here. It's all rather horrid, and I don't like thinking about it much."

22.5.88

"Peter, to hark back to your life in Washington, you have never told us your name, family name, nor christian name, or that of your parents. You filled in a lot of details, but not names, apart from your rich patron. This seems strange."

"Well it was a long time ago, and at the level we were at names did not mean much. It was:

'Here you nigger!'

However, I will have a think back and let you know. Also your relationship to me at that time."

22.5.88

"I would like to say more about the life as Memstec."

"Is that a name Peter?"

"Yes."

"Christian name?"

"Yes. Not sure I know. Have lots of memories of June as Harriet."

"Good memories?"

"Yes."

"That's nice!"

"She fought for me."

"Still doing it in this life, Pete! I always thought you were worth fighting for."

"Lots of memories too of Michael as well."

"Why is that, can you explain?"

"I believe Michael realises why."

"I believe he has got ideas. What was Michael's relation in this life?"

"Mother. Know I loved my mum."

12.8.88

"You were asking about life before the Washington period into which I was born... Well it seems that you dad, as a female black, were born in the south to a slave family that worked for a planter. As you know, slaves were treated very badly in those areas and you were no exception. Mum was the daughter of the planter, and was somewhat older than you.

When the planter died of drink she came into ownership of the plantation; she sold up, having freed the slaves, and moved to Washington with a small fortune. She became very unpopular with the other planters in the south because she freed her slaves, and that set a bad example, so she virtually had to move north.

You came with her as her personal maid, having married my father, and I was born in the north, free but still under prejudice as a black. You were about eighteen when the planter died, and had a very hard time with him and the plantation overseer before the breakup came. Enforced sex, whippings, etc. so you were very grateful to mum for having rescued you from all that."

16.1.89

"I see I caused a lot of heartache then. I resented the lack of respect shown to my mother, of whom I was very fond. She was much more intelligent than rich people gave her credit. Some folk tried to rope her in to their resourceful ways of spending much of their time. I tried to use my guile to save her problems but she thought it more important that I kept a good character, than that I helped her protect herself.

The rich men thought they should be able to use her body at will. She never refused outright, but she mostly saw to it that she had other things of importance to do."

"This is why you are saying she was much more intelligent, more subtle in handling situations than you wanted to be."

"I think some help was given by Harriet."

"She brought her favourite slave from the south and released her, and so she wanted to protect her."

"I don't think she approved of her husband's friends."

"You have never said anything about Harriet's husband."

"I feel the time is not right. I will say more when dictates make it appropriate."

"Are you carrying on about the Washington life?"

"I question which trial I intended to handle in that life. I landed with so many resentments in the end that no real progress appears to have been made. I tried to respond to care from Harriet."

"She tried to help from what you said before."

"But every time I tried to make progress it seemed it was foiled by a misunderstanding because I was black."

"It still goes on in much of the world Pete."

"I was lucky to be released. I don't think my mother saw it that way!"

19.1.89

"I want to talk more about my life as Memstec. Most common folk in those days had reason to question God's existence. I questioned that such a being really could allow such unfairness between a morphosis. I know now that the reason I lived that life was to die rampageously! Mostly folk then died of starvation, which caused other physical problems leading to an early death."

"Are you talking about the black community?"

"Yes."

"I imagine many did not live a long life."

"I knew that reason would not apply in my life. I could feed well. We initially had freedom to use our skills. Later Harriet looked after our needs."

"So you weren't hungry. Presumably you were experiencing other aspects of your class?"

"A lot depended on my acceptance of my position in life. This I found difficult."[1]

Charles Pizzey   Life No.2

21.1.88

Peter says he remembered when a small boy that he had once had another life. Asked what memories he had, he replied:~

"Principally that I died young, 37 years, as a butler in Chelsea."

7.2.88

Peter drew attention to a Victorian photograph album claiming he had been Charles Pizzey, and putting names to many of the photographs:~

"I have started to go back in lives with Charles being the first to look at."

1   A factor in life no. 2, as Charles Pizzey.

13.2.88

Asked if he was still going through the life as Charles Pizzey, he replied:~

"Yes, it's not always in order. Sometimes we go to an earlier stage and see how this influences the result in a later stage."

"I suppose in the end you will come to some conclusion about how well you managed that life, what the successes and failures were?"

"Yes. I suppose that is to come. It is all a bit shattering at times, when one sees how badly one behaved, and what opportunities were missed."

"You must have been through all these details after you died in that life?"

"Yes, that's true. But it helps the assessment of this last life to go back to the previous one and check whether characteristics which needed to be changed were actually experienced and successfully overcome in the last life, or not. So for that reason we go through previous lives."

"I never did like post examination analysis, filled me with horror at school!"

"Yes, this is almost worse, because it shows how important living life correctly is, and how poorly most of us respond. No wonder our school-days drag on and we return term after term to Earth."

9.6.88

Peter explained that Charles had started work at Plumstead aged 12, repairing horse reins (1872/3). He quoted several areas in London to which he had moved. His work included cleaning of lavatories:~

"I told you I started my 'Charles life' as decidedly insignificant. Don't know about washing floors, but I used to clean out disgusting loos!"

22.2.88

"I can recall more of my life in Church Street and what happened about that time. The recollections go on gradually. I am not forced in any way to go over them, but from time to time the feeling grows that I could just go back and relive that bit. So I do, and though some bits are rather painful, I feel afterwards that is a lesson learnt and I shall not have to repeat that again.

Funny how during the re-run I seem to feel the effect of what I did, like an echo rebounding from a rock face time and time again, until it finally dies away, the effect on other people's lives."

24.2.88

"Ellen, my wife, was almost prostrate after I collapsed and died in the pub. I choked to death because I had another whiskey when I had a very heavy cold and things got blocked. It was very quickly over for me. I was just so sorry for Ellen and the family."

Peter explained that Charles had worked at Church Street, Chelsea, 'just doing odd jobs'. He was there about ten years. Asked if he had worked his way up in the household:~

"Yes, because the old butler trained me. He was ill for a long time, and I did the job."

He explained how Ellen came to work there and they eventually got married:~

"Ellen became housekeeper at Church Street, we married and left to run a pub at Highbury. I was 26 and she was 30."

25.2.88

"How did you come in contact with Royalty; you have photographs of some of them in the album?"

"Well, there were visits to the house in Church St. from members of Royalty. There was an occasional dinner for the Prince and Princess. That was a great occasion, and we were quite exhausted afterwards. Other servants were brought in to help, and things were chaotic I remember. I managed to get photos of the royal guests for my album."

"Can you remember who lived at Church Street?"

"No, can't remember all their names."

"Well, what was the family name?"

"Bowes I think, but couldn't be sure."

"Were you the butler at these dinners?"

"Not the only one. Others were brought in. Quite a lot of extra staff."

14.4.88

Concerning the difficulty in accepting his position in life, which led to a drinking problem:~

"I think I know why I died young. I behaved in a mad sort of way."

"In respect of what?"

"Drink. As Charles I again started in a poor situation, but I worked this time with improvement in mind. This I achieved young but had

137

no real family support. So I 'supported' myself by drinking too much once I had acquired responsibilities which I found too great a load."

"A frequent pitfall! You must have worked your way up without resorting to that support?"

"Yes, unfortunately I found it was the way rich people coped. I did not then appreciate the pitfalls. As I told you before, I reached a low condition and it was not making good use of Earth time so I departed. Question is whether I achieved what I intended to do. I feel I had hoped to cope better with taking responsibility. There was a built-in escape route to my life. I did not want to collect people's disapproval. This is eventually inevitable if you allow drink to take a disproportionate place in life."

27.1.89

Having been speaking of life as a judge (life no. 4) I commented that having held responsibility, handling this still seemed to have been a pitfall for Charles:~

"In that life as Charles I was responsible to others, not a law unto myself. Some of the problem was financial. I had difficulties in managing money and needed a very determined wife to assist the process, but Ellen was a bad manager of money as well."

4.5.89

"Charles was not really terribly happy. A lot of his effort went into gaining prestige rather than a more constructive type of experience. He was much deluded by grandeur. He intended to pass on his inner understanding of truth, as well as proving his ability to become respected, when a somewhat decadent start was made. I refer to his parentage which was scarcely grand. In that respect he succeeded, but not in handing on his knowledge of truth. You see he tried to handle too much at once, without the support of strong family ties. Robert (his father) had his own problems."

1.7.89

"A lot of his problem was because he thought a lot of himself, evidently determined to become someone of importance. You see he had experienced being on the receiving end of racist feelings in his earlier life. He tried to prove then that he equated superior position with intelligence and hard work, and could not reconcile what he saw and heard very often with these gifts.

He needed to be approved of by society, and felt that to start from scratch and work hard and be servile when necessary, must enable one to be respected and finally raise oneself to the top position.

I completely overlooked the responsibility that goes with that position.

I do not think I could have lasted as a butler, because I became very disenchanted. The usual pattern of behaviour I perceived, was laisse faire once one was in the top position. Nobody cared about the consequences of their actions. They were generally able to abuse their position without consequential problems. I of course had done just that in an earlier life, but my abuse had been of a different nature. I had then thought that I was a pillar of society.

Many of the people Charles met were not engaged in efforts to improve society's ills. Mostly they were only using time in the manner that their position allowed. I saw that I could not tolerate the need to keep my position by smiling benignly as I ordered the smooth running of their orgies. I knew they did not really appreciate the hard work which was involved in the smooth running of events to which a big individual application of manual labour had to be given.

If any member failed, the system ran into problems. Hence, tension was high, but there was no question of striking for a different body of rules. I certainly learned the art of being servile but usually was less than happy. Beneath the surface I longed for true respect for my person, not just for my organising ability.

I of course could not have continued unless I forwent marriage. I had the idea that the pub would give me proper recognition, and leave me free to be myself. I did not reckon with other problems in plenty. I could not handle them. I was by then geared to asking for appropriate wherewithal, not sorting out how I provided all that was required. I suppose the experience showed up my lack of determination in difficult circumstances."

Summary of life as Charles Pizzey   20.10.89

In this summary Peter reveals the thread that inter-connects the patterns of previous lifes:~

"Charles started life in freedom, and a lot of his background had previously been in servile situations. He had known what slavery had meant as an American negro (life no.3). In this life he had graduated to a position of implied acceptance. But he had understood that position did not necessarily render one free. As a Roman overseer (life no. 8), he had been anything but free to follow his inclinations. As a judge (life no.4), he was servant to the state in which he lived. As he was later to discover, he could not exercise freedom as a servant, even when he held the esteem of the household, and in material terms the status of having control of other staff. A great deal depended on the master, or as he would now prefer to be called, the head of department.

Just what does constitute freedom? It is the ability to listen and respond to the 'still small voice' within one's being. This is the permanent atom which resides within our hearts when we are in a physical body, and which constitutes our eternal self. Until we can hear and respond to this essence of our very spiritual existence, we continue to struggle with characteristics which govern our responses to the world around us.

Charles struggled to be his inner self, to handle responsibility, to be worthy of trust, and at the same time express his love and concern for others around him. But propriety demanded certain standards be met, regardless of the suffering imposed on others, or the debasement of spiritual understanding, which some would have liked to make the guiding principle of their life and work. I feel that Charles had been well aware of these difficulties before he incarnated.

As a supervisor of smuggling operations, he had tried to be responsible and fair-minded. The need for self-discipline was not a characteristic mastered by many with whom he was associated. The pressing need, both of money and self-preservation, caused him to abandon principles he needed to exercise. His aims were not fulfilled, he died having made little spiritual progress.

His life as a judge gave him considerable power, and little freedom. Again, he had to fulfil an indescribable reactionary role if he were to gain, and hold, the respect of the governing hierarchy. He considered his own material well-being, completely abandoning his commitment to respond to his inner consciousness.

As a negro, he tried to hold on to fair-mindedness, and was taught that as an insignificant, you experience the same problem of listening and following the dictates of your true self.

I think, because Charles knew of the pitfalls, he had built in an escape route for operating should expression of true self become smothered by exigencies of life on earth. Hence, repetition of denigration of spirit would not cause further backsliding.

Please rethink your acceptance of reincarnation as a realistic way forward having re-read the characteristics of my past lives."

Peter Cowlin

Life No.1
2.9.87

This detailed review of Peter's last incarnation reveals how a life is reviewed, the depth of this process, and the lessons and observations about one's life as they compare to the life plan devised before conception:~

"Hello Pete."

"My schooling, the Steiner part anyway, was one of the best parts of my life. I enjoyed being with other young people. The holidays were terrific also. Some things I didn't enjoy so much; the ATC, the court appearance. Still, taking it all together it was an enjoyable life.

"Pity it had to end so abruptly!"

"Yes, I hope I'll know the answer to that sometime."

1.11.87

"You seem to be growing in maturity rapidly, Pete."

"Yes, I suppose I am picking up the parts of me that didn't come to Earth last time, and joining them together to make a whole. I am free to expand my thoughts here. There is no restriction on them."

"Have you started the review of your last life?"

"Yes, in part. I've faced some of the difficult bits. The life sits there like a model railway, complete in itself, but having sections, stations, bridges, level crossings, all of which one can see at a glance. You can take a train forward or backward, and stop to admire, or be horrified, at any given point. Why did I do this or that action just then? What effect did it have on others? You feel the effect in full measure, bad or good.

This can be rewarding or appalling, and one can be encouraged or thrown into despair. The way forward is clear: where one has failed, this must be undergone again in some distant future, and one must try once more, as one had tried in the past in so many lives to overcome and succeed.

No, I haven't had much contact with past lives, no doubt this is to come. One just feels on certain issues that this is something one has tried for so many times in the past, but unsuccessfully as in this last life, and one kicks oneself yet again. I refer, of course, to the car episode, material possessions, flouting of the rules, defying authority, all elements to be faced and accepted."

14.12.87

"Pete, do you reckon you achieved all of what you intended to do in your last life?"

"Well, that's a big question! Probably not. On the other hand I think that the time at the two Steiner schools made such a change in the way I was thinking that must have been part of what I meant to do. I think if I had been able to go on to help others more in my work after school, that would have been something else I meant to do – Pete."

16.12.87

"What have you learned about life in your last visit here, Pete?"

"Well! I suppose what happens if one goes against authority. Also, how stuck in their ideas most people are; the Steiner school taught me that one has to ask questions, the right questions, to get to the truth, or towards the truth. But, it was when I got here that I discovered how little one knows on Earth, and how much there is to know – Pete."

12.1.88

"I've started going back over the last life in detail. It began by a feeling that I ought to see how I did and I found myself almost taken out of myself in a dream or reverie. A picture in 3-d appeared of a babe which was me. There seemed to be a feeling of sadness around which alarmed me. Later there was the meeting with you and mum. I was getting uncertain at this time, but something told me that you were to be my home. I was much happier when you took me.

Then I was in my own little room. Someone I couldn't see was with me during this vision, and told me this was a time of decision in my life. But, the decision was not mine, it was other people's, and the effect was fear that it might not be the right one. It was though, and the fear and sadness went, and I was very happy.

Well, I am through the baby stage now, and a small boy growing up. I was obviously into everything. Very fond of 'Mopsy' basset. I was very interested in everything; needed some watching!

The sessions do not seem to go on for long. After a bit they fade, and I am back to normal life here – Pete."

19.1.88

"I have been reliving primary school, at least the start. I feel frustration all round, though I tried my best. That awful day when I set fire to paper in the toilet, and then ran away, and hid in the car!

142

Everyone searching for me; fear, and a determination not to be caught!"

23.1.88

"How are things this morning?"

"Very comfortable. I feel bathed in this warm light. Just reclining here, no worries, except what I will have to repeat on the next lot of the review! Then I get great support, no criticism, from the presence that is with me. I would just like to kick myself sometimes, doesn't work so well with a thought body!"

"Still Pete, this is the whole point of a life on Earth isn't it? If one doesn't make mistakes, one can't learn."

"Yes, I know that, but I seem to make such large errors. I wonder why, now?"

"Well, the errors were not totally yours Pete. Others must share the responsibility by causing the situation to which you reacted."

"Ah! But it is the way I reacted that counts, and that depended on the way I looked at the events that went before. I see that now. I see also an echo from previous lives when I reacted in a similar way to similar events. My attitude changed when I was thrown into Steiner, in a world that was so different. The best decision I made in that life was to go to the Steiner school and I think that came from my higher self, with the help of a particular member of the school staff."

"Well, you made it didn't you?. That's what makes your life so very worth while."

30.1.88

"How far have you got with your life review?"

"The Steiner school, it was a tremendous opening up for me. A sort of expansion of consciousness. A sudden awakening to a new view of life.

I wondered what on earth I was doing learning about literature, poems, myths of the Norsemen, and so on. Some things like mathematics did not come at all easily, and I had endless arguments with some of the teachers. But, I could develop myself without being squashed by someone.

New friends too were a great stimulus in much better directions. Neil and Craig were great, and I had a lot of fun. So life blossomed, and I really enjoyed my time in Kent.

My thoughts on the realities of life developed, and a lecture confirmed what you had talked about in those early meetings at home which I taped. So that prepared me for the change."

6.2.88

"Why did your life have to terminate when it did?"

"Well, it was tied up with my previous life which was not as successful as had been hoped. Despite opportunities then I did not make provision for my family, or as much provision as I could, and died of drink leaving a struggling wife and children.

This time I was determined not to be consumed by alcohol, and do better. Had I gone on beyond Kings Langley, I would have been faced with much greater difficulties. I might have been gaoled for dangerous driving, or something. As it was I left at a high spot."

"But, why the bike accident, and not some other way?"

"Well there could have been other ways. It seems the favoured was a climbing or caving accident, which in some ways might have been more acceptable. Whichever way it seems a head injury was the chosen method, and long before the accident I sort of felt this intuitively.

Now due to the Steiner influence, which is still very strong with me, I have a whole new opportunity to open to spiritual knowledge, and I intend to make the most of it before I have to go to Earth again. In fact, by working hard, I can probably delay descent to Earth life for some time."

16.3.88

"Most people on Earth Dad, have little or no idea that there exists a plan for their lives. So their chances of being able to fulfil that plan voluntarily are naturally rather slim. However, as you know from teachings, the soul holds that plan, and those few on Earth who are guided by their souls will stand a much greater chance of fulfilling their plan, provided they are truly guided, and do not let their personality take over the guidance.

As you also know, spiritual healing tends to bridge the gap between soul and personality, so the soul can regain command, which it had at birth but lost in the course of Earthly education."

"What's it like for you Pete?"

"Well, this last life (no.1), I managed to span the gap fairly well towards the end, I think, thanks to the Steiner school's influence, but it was touch and go. Had I not gone to the Kent school the outcome would have been quite different.

We need to look at our experiences in a given life so that we can arrange for the next one to provide the experiences we lack, or have not handled well."

16.12.88

"I know you were very irritated by my lying in bed. I question whether my motives for lying in bed were justified."

"Your motives at that time were to avoid boring school, and do something more rewarding."

"I realise my pattern of work left much to be desired. Very often my motives were bad. I thought the people concerned with my education were all against me as a person."

"So, if we incarnate and need to do various things, and the system on Earth forces you in the wrong direction, you should comply and not show displeasure!"

"Question of taking opportunities. I know sometimes it's necessary to have detrimental experiences in order to grow."

"Yes, this is clearly shown in your young life, and if you hadn't kicked at schooling and what followed, you would not have arrived at a Steiner School which raised your level."

22.12.88

Peter comments on recent Earth tragedies and consequent emotional and physical traumas, and emphasises the importance of understanding one's objective:~

"That is experience. It's a case of trying to apply a different set of values, of understanding the reason for having to cope with such a situation."

"I do understand this Pete, in theory. In practise it is very difficult to be part of current Earth life, and hold those views. Very, very few people can put these theories into practise."

"I question some people's objectives in life. A lot of people's sole objective is to acquire material things, and have pleasure. I very often thought life was just for pleasure. But, then a great number of different experiences made me feel there must be a reason connecting them. I found odd things happened to me."

"You were beginning to be aware of higher consciousness."

"For example, I could not understand why I took cars. I felt there must be a purpose behind it. It could be connected with my life as a judge." (See 13.1.89 below).

"I see it as the other side of the coin. Amongst other things, it led you to the Steiner connection. Made a big step for you."

4.1.89

Assessing the purpose of the past lives recalled, Peter said:~

"There is a lot of reasons to think that lives have purpose. The reason I reincarnated so soon (died 1899, reborn 1969) was because bad influences had taken over in the earlier life, as Charles, and barred me achieving anything useful then. The bad influences had created an irretrievable situation."

"What were they?"

"A great deal was to do with drink. I knew when I returned here that I had done nothing towards getting to grips with my very apparent problems, not drink, but the personality defects which occasioned the need."

"How would you describe those difficulties."

"A lack of determination in overcoming difficult situations."

"So you gave yourself 'dutch courage', as the saying goes. That approach to life is very common."

"I determined to overcome this weakness, I must make that point clear. I found that, as Peter, I was drawn to whiskey at a very early age; it had been the favoured drink to consume for Charles."

"On your last New Year's Eve on Earth you had a small whiskey, but only drank a sip of it. The rest I found in the morning!"

"I had begun to feel a repugnant reaction to all spirit. Because I died like I did, the memory of whiskey was still there! I realised I had lived before, but I still did not recall the circumstances."

13.1.89

Peter explains the need for what may otherwise appear as unacceptable behaviour:~

"I think my aberration about cars was connected with doubt about my ability to find out how one became entwined with criminals unless one joined them. When I was young you used to tell me the principles of moral living. I knew I remembered other standards, and I could not see why this should be.

Like most young children I wanted to understand, because I knew a lot of good did actually exist where people condemned others. *I had to have first hand knowledge of how, so-called, crime begins.*

The difficulty was I really hated everything to do with crime. I dreaded punishment. I wanted to wander in the country which I loved, but that would just have put off the evil day. Mind you time seemed to rely on tragedy catching up. I knew early on that until radical steps were taken, I would not complete the trauma, and that the time allowed was short.

If I became overly studious, the chance of tackling the experience would be much reduced. I could have backed off, and enjoyed, amongst other things, a good deal of support from the establishment. That was an attractive bit to refute. Sometimes I felt like succumbing.

Because at the Steiner school one was expected, as here, to learn about oneself, I was given the opportunity to recapture some of my real self again. This made a big difference when I came here. A criminal record, even if for the purpose of experience, takes time to overcome in terms of complete rehabilitation. I needed a little time."

31.1.89

"At the Kings Langley Steiner school I had already sensed I would not be around long, so it was in a way less purposeful (than the Kent school), though there were some very positive aspects to those months, and I again was very happy there."

"We feel that too, and there were certain people you seemed to need contact with."

"I know some were connected with other lives. It helped me to realise my connection was not just my imagination."

"Your feeling of other lives you mean?"

"I tried to think how you fitted in, but I could not remember any connection between you and some of the people I felt I had known before."

"Any clearer now?"

"Yes, I feel most of the Steiner folk have links with Atlantis, and the very fact you came to know about Steiner when you did went a long way towards my renewing this contact with them."

"Obviously it was the vital link. Had we not come across Steiner schooling, a vital link would have been missing."

"I think the key is to never miss an opportunity."

1.2.89

"I like to think I have made some progress in my life as Peter. I realise I had found my intended family, but I only wish we merged like this on Earth. I used to make many difficulties then, but I must say a lot of them were for a purpose. I like to think I behaved well at other times."

"You were delightful Peter, very often."

"I meant to give pleasure to other people."

"You gave a great deal of pleasure, more than you thought at times."

"There were several sorts of requirements in that life. For example, I needed to learn to make relationships with some of the types of people I had so despised in other lives. I found many old associations amongst my acquaintances.

I deliberately turned away from those I truly admired to become part of the 'other group'. They were not bad at heart, just learning like the rest of us, but not conforming by Earth standards. I had to relate to them by eventually trying to lead them. Sometimes this was quite something; a question of making an impression by overwhelming with apparent knowledge.

I knew I did not want to end up a lay-about. I needed to try to understand why they chose to attempt to progress along particular paths, and realised I must do something that would be considered in their province. So I chose the less mundane way of crossing society; like to think a decidedly less harmful way than many."

"Turned out to be fairly harmless."

"But I question whether making some effort to impress my associates was really worthwhile. They had not intended to get into serious trouble this time round. I felt I really wanted to be in control of my actions; I really was past behaving with the crowd mentality.

I think I learned some insight into behaviour, such as how others react to certain misdemeanours. I must say most do not think of any action as experience."

"Yes, but not seen in that way on Earth. Some say that they hope the lesson has been learned, but not meaning it in your sense."

"I want to look at other aspects of the life."

11.2.89

"In giving more information about my last life, I hope it will help you to understand why I behaved in so many strange ways."

"Well, at Earth level, it was difficult to understand at the time why particular patterns were emerging."

"Do not feel I was in any way unhappy. I gave that impression at one stage to a lot of people. I see I was much discussed at school. You were not asked for your opinion very much. This is frequently a failing of modern psychology. People think they can argue better if those that are closest are not involved to evaluate their conclusions.

You even began to wonder if I wanted to live elsewhere. That was because I took off from primary school several times."

"It did start to become a little incomprehensible! We were under pressure of authority trying to stop the happenings."

"I realise the difficulty was that the system demands unquestionable toeing of the accepted line, otherwise everyone considers what is wrong with the child, or else blames the parents for lack of control. No one once considers that the child may need the experience, and the parent does not have the option of crushing that completely, even if they are right in assessing it as dangerous.

You were very concerned that I might become one of the police statistics as a murder victim. That of course was because social work made you very aware of these dangers. Now I think you can appreciate it was not part of the plan. I had experienced death at someone else's hand in a much earlier life; we all do at some time. For a few people this is desired in childhood. For the majority it is an experience they choose to have later in life. I like to think you do now realise we all plan our lives before we arrive on Earth. Much more is done these days to thwart one's plans, in good faith. I can assure you that if actions deprive people of the experience they want, it's an irritation felt when this is assessed here."

"I can see that Pete."

"Please do not think I felt this. You saw my need for different kinds of titillation. You also saw where crossing the line could lead me, something we do try to take into account when planning our incarnation, and a point at which some plans go awry. It goes to show how I just kept to the right side until I'd made time for handling criminal knowledge more possible. What I'm really trying to say is I needed to make the risks I took more intelligible to me by virtue of previous experience."

Peter continues to talk about the life plan devised before birth and how it can often include non-conformist behaviour. He indicates that once all the facets of behaviour are linked and resolved, one can begin to contact the totality of one's being, or true Self:~

"I think we always attempt to make plans, and are thrown when it is disturbed. It can sometimes be useful, but it's a question of having faith in ourselves.

I want to talk about my last life. I made the decision to become difficult, so to speak, when I reached the age of eight."

"Are you saying you made the decision before you were born?"

"Yes, I knew I had the choice of either doing very well, at my intellectual pursuits, and becoming an additional name on the register of stable personalities, or breaking out, and experiencing many facets of uncontrolled reasoning."

"You mean you made this choice before incarnating?"

"Yes, I realised I needed, at some time, to tie up loose ends once and for all. This had impressed itself on me, because I had not linked in with a favourable group the last time round."

"Are you talking about an Earth group?"

"Yes."

"Favourable in what way?"

"I had not been involved then in anything but orthodox Christianity, and that was of little avail for spiritual progress. You see in lives long ago, I had experienced much of what you are using today. I refer to healing and psychotherapy. I was helped by these methods, and went on to study them myself."

"Lives a long time ago?"

"For example, I would have made little progress by becoming a much admired replica of Dr Johnston."

"Which one?"

"I refer to literary prowess, or come to that medical prowess; it's all the same. It amounts to adoration of common achievement in Earth terms. People respect that kind of progress, often only because a high standard of living is also achieved.

But then it's a question of how one employs one's skills. Most people are too exhausted by their daily toil to bother much about any deep study outside their profession. They give their lives to doing a good job and then resting on their laurels. Such a life can be pleasurable, but they realise when they return here little progress has been made.

I had spent several lives learning about failure in respect of taking responsibility in how I handled the ultimate outcome of a given situation. I knew I needed to understand more positively about how to approach unacceptable behaviour. It was time to clinch the radical code of conduct, which I shall not need to repeat.

I have started to join these experiences to my total self. Once they are linked by full knowledge and acceptance of the positive and negative aspects of my behaviour, the same link will now be for ever with me, and can henceforth be used in a positive way."

"Peter, you are saying that a lot of your Self is left on your side when you come down?"

"I shall not leave out the important aspect of my ability to discipline my own behaviour again."

17.4.89

Concerning a progression in consciousness from one's early origin:~

"The only reason for experiencing past lives is to understand more about your current one. This understanding can come from other things, for example it can come as a paradigm shift of consciousness. This usually happens following an experience that deeply affects you.

I would like to tell you about a big change that took place in my progress round the circle of the zodiac common to average man travelling in space and time. I now find I am going to travel in the reverse direction.[1] This means I have completed a phase of development, a historical journey through the zodiac.

Now I must seek progress in another system of nature's massive network of life's aspirations. I feel the idea of a reversal of energies used may add good vibrations to one's abilities. I have much more to investigate."

"How do you know this reversal is going to happen?"

"I find I had planned a zodiacal gyration long ago."

"Don't think I understand really. From another life, one doesn't go from one sign to the next automatically?"

"It is done that way at a very early stage of acquiring both experience and control. I am thinking in aeons of time. Later, one must acquire the right energies for progress of one's characteristics."

---

1   An astrological reference to the so-called *Path of return*, applicable to a spiritually awakened person.

"One's mind boggles at that prospect, getting everything together, and finding the right source is beyond our conception."

"A good deal of help is available at that complicated time if one asks for guidance. Because one needs all the experiences from different introspective stances, it could be manifested in behaviour of a loving nature under any manner of personalities. Copious possibilities exist. We need therefore not be so specific in our timing, and can concentrate more on finding the right environment."

"Does that make it less complicated?"

"Yes, I feel I have opened up another area for exploration."

"By us, or by you?"

"By you. Ponder on what I have said."

30.4.89

"I have been doing a lot of thinking, questioning myself closely regarding my motives. Often I made reasons for my behaviour that were quite incongruous. I don't think you believed I told deliberate lies, but my imagination was such that I deluded *myself* as to my motives. I often did things that I felt I had to do for no particularly good reason, except that I felt spurred on by some inner need.

I expect people would say I failed to consider the consequences of my behaviour, or else that I lacked ability to discriminate. It was neither, I was driven by a deeper portion of my psyche. It must be the same for many who seem to indulge in unreasonable plans.

Please give out this thought to others. It is important to see purpose in all behaviour. I know now it is linked to a plan much greater in purpose than just succeeding in a particular line. That is really ultimately of little consequence in itself. Sometimes one's needs make one follow a course that is not against the image society considers it can label as 'successful'. At other times, personal need for growth of spirit is such that a totally disreputable life serves a purpose better. I hope this makes sense to you."

"Yes, a difficult concept to get across."

"But, it is very, very important in terms of society having a different outlook on what happens. Beyond a certain point, resistance will always be met unless people hold a concept of eternity. I realise that at the time you had not got the insight in this way."

"That's quite true Peter, one hadn't been involved to the same extent. We would still have had concern for you because of society's reaction. There are considerable hazards attached to living these difficult lives."

Summary of life as Peter

"My initial reaction to looking at the whole span of Peter's life again is one of joy. I feel that I accomplished more than I thought originally. I see how much I was given simply by being taken into your care. I am really very grateful that you had so much belief in people learning self-control.

Like so many children, I tried most of the arguments about the way I thought things should go. I seldom went undetected. When I faltered I was aware of the displeasure I incurred and at a young age became saddened by my apparent lack of responsibility towards others. I must have seemed totally devoid of consideration.

I tried to give everybody the impression I was completely self-sufficient. I think only you realised someone totally different was the real me. I wish I could have been able to be the real me, and yet get the experiences that I needed in order to make a considerable inroad into my progression in the permanent world. My feeling is that I have made a considerable move in the right direction.

I shall list the things which had a direct bearing on my development from 'sinner' to 'saint'. Not that I have become the latter, but I use the analogy to try to make an important point. You see, when behaviour warrants more trouble from future lives, it cannot be deemed to be learned within the psyche, only coped with superficially. We all tend to land eventually with numerous bits and pieces which we have struggled with for aeons of time, without really putting them quite behind us. I was one of those who had failed to complete some specially vital aspects of character control on other occasions. I could so easily have slipped up again, I could even have slipped back, had I not left Earth at a high point in my achievements.

Life on Earth is quite relentless in its attack on one's inherent weaknesses, and one requires to consolidate one's gains by working for the good of others from here. This dedication cements us, not only in spirit, but in such a bond that it cannot be broken, but only grazed in future lives. So it is of considerable relief to be able to look back on horrendous upheavals in earlier lives, and know that I shall not lack the same abilities which caused such mishandling of possible opportunities for being of service to others.

I shall hope to spend less time struggling against accepted standards of behaviour knowing from the start that I have a duty to help make more commendable practices a common inherent part of Earth experience.

This is quite difficult to explain in simple terms, actually more difficult than I had envisaged. I feel I may try to put it another way as well. It really is of such vital importance that people know how development takes place.

It really is not a case of luck or chance, we all need to cope with the same flaws in our make-up. How we respond depends solely on the stage of our development. But it is not even as simple as that, because everyone has individuality, and therefore has an individual way of trying to learn.

Of course, for some, little insight seems to be acquired. Hence the same mistakes pass over them without being appreciated for what they are. I suppose this must have been so for many of us in the past. I cannot explain quite how such differences still exist. Maybe Spirit not only did not manifest all at once, but maybe some portion slumbered. I just do not understand, and can only say differences are considerable.

Like most young people in the present part of the 20th century, Peter arrived in the western world, as it is known, at a time of plenty. I do not solely refer to food, though this he enjoyed. After all, he had been well schooled in provisions, both food and drink, as Charles. He had then not lacked material comforts in later life. Creature comforts had held some attraction for him but Peter lived in an age of infinitely more opportunity for varied experiences. Schools were involved in science and much craft, both of which were of crucial importance to him. Both were subjects of which he had no recent experience. Science was quite awe inspiring in its modern form. He needed to have opportunity to discover its many facets, and craft gave opportunity for expression of inner concepts.

He did not recall personal details of (his) other lives but sometimes felt sympathy for other's lives, particularly those in problem with authority. Do not infer that he admired the depravity which he sometimes encountered on film, if not in person. He knew so much was not what it appeared to be. He knows now the truth behind such feeling. At Earth-level he could only seek to understand through experience.

On many occasions Peter fell foul of authority. He found it difficult to accept that he was receiving wisdom that was appropriate to his needs. He questioned the ultimate aim of education in relation to his reincarnation. He knew that he could attempt to follow only in order to please, rather than because he felt it was important for his progress. He seldom found that arguments for restricting activities to those justified by a requirement of social respectability, satisfied his need to experience pragmatic truths. He realised his life was not to be long, and that the question of getting some better understanding of problems was involved. He sensed he must gather some threads together in his understanding of other people's problems which he had questioned previously.

I know one's port of call must be clear before much progress can be made. I like to think that I came to Earth last time with a clear vision of what I wanted to achieve, and with a blueprint of how the process needed to be developed.

I see now how easy it is for others to mar the way. A lot depends on influence from this side of life, as you term it. It depends, in other words, on Earth folk listening to what you call the 'still, small voice' inside your head, or evidence of intuition, which is still not regarded highly in your beliefs.

I was fortunate in having made firm links with discarnate friends, and had the good fortune to arrive at the intended destination. From this juncture I could pursue my adopted course. I realise now how very important it is to arrive where other influences are likely to provide appropriate openings for experiences, and how important it is to chose parents who are developing outlooks that can be opportune in lending scope for manoeuvre. I found I had made the right choice.

Of course, others were involved at the time of decision but had long since forgotten the plan. However, a degree of intuitive memory had remained, and was a vital ingredient of the process. I refer to my desire to be an adopted son at a specific period in history, and a specific period in my chosen parents' life. I would not wish you to conclude that the options were obvious to me by the time I had finally reached my family, but I can assure you I knew I had arrived as planned.

Perhaps no particular help actually could benefit my progress from then on had I lost complete contact with my innermost being. I most certainly had forgotten my plan by the time I could talk, but within me I felt a compunction to follow a course of action that deviated frequently from the norm. In this process to which I have already referred, I actually learned to handle many of my outstanding character disparities.

I guess however I frame my words, doubt about my statements will remain. Add to this my deliberate platitudes. I intend now to end by only giving my gains in a materially comprehensive way. I have managed to handle with reasonable success the following things that had bedevilled me for aeons of time. Remember I have already said that to cope successfully with these character traits, one has to control them from within, not be in superficial control. We all run this course.

I believe I can now set behind me: drink, drugs, greed, self-oriented gain for its own sake, a resentment of authority, a lack of trust in others, and a lack of belief in myself.

I could rephrase that and say:

'I feel I have learned the ability to trust in myself.'

This can only happen, not as a result of outstanding achievement, but when one acknowledges the existence of one's true Self, which is always within. It is our indestructible core and dictates our every action with fortitude. It knows mistakes will be made; that does not matter. Love can heal, but only if we acknowledge that love is deep within us all, all the time."

10. Communications From Other Folk

About communication, Experiences on arrival, Ways of helping others, The problem of communicating with Earth folk, One's character an open book, Review of previous incarnations, Summary – Linking lives in groups, Giving thought to changing priorities.

This chapter contains a small selection of observations which are relevant to understanding personal experiences, lessons, and development after death.

Apart from our son's communications, others have come to this channel. Some we have known as family or friends from many years ago; others have established a past contact of limited duration.

Some say they have a link through friends or associates; others have no Earth connection but have wanted to lend their support to communication. Then there have been those from earlier generations who have endeavoured to establish their family connections. The decision to communicate was theirs alone, perhaps they were spurred on by Peter's enthusiasm 'to prove life goes on and has purpose'.

Apart from the family members helping to join the threads of serial lives, there was a facet common to all. Most were anxious to give a picture of their own well-being, and of an environment very different from that generally envisaged as the 'realm of the dead'. There was often a desire to let earthbound relatives know this. They were wanting to talk, leaving undeniable impressions of their individual characters, supported by the readily recognisable manner of expression of those known personally. The experience suggests that no drastic change takes place immediately on death.

About communication   2.4.89

Peter implies the impact that acceptance of the possibility of communication, of survival after death and of help would have to world affairs:~

"I want to talk about communication. I feel so much depends on its acceptance. I do not only mean a great deal of heartache is possibly saved but I also feel that the establishment of this useful tool could make a big difference to the eventual outcome of world affairs. You see, Man's mind would become differently oriented. It would not necessarily stop him using his free will to destroy, or for gaining power, but he might have more positive opposition to various actions and a better balance could result.

I realise the very mention of help from here is scorned by the mainstream of homo sapiens. I know this is a result of Man's total rejection of a boss who is all-loving, as well as all-powerful, but that choice was consciously made and readily accepted by the majority, so now the result must be handled.

I see the question of life continuing as of vital importance in the outcome. I want to try my best to have a positive effect on Man's thought. I realise that some will always reject. Even influencing a small proportion could help develop a means of rejuvenating the planet for people to continue to use in time to come."

Experiences on arrival

A Primary School Teacher   19.12.88

"I want you to tell people that death resembles a forest trail."
"That's a fascinating concept."
"Every time you look there is something fresh to see."

Ned (a family friend)   17.1.89

"Everybody doubts that life continues. I used to think I would perhaps sit in some kind of residence, with angels all trumpeting beautiful music."

"So you had a picture which you felt indicated that you were going to exist. What have you found?"

"I find I am totally muddled. Trouble is I am quite ignorant about so much."

"Can you describe what happened for you on your passing?"

"I came to the realisation I had died when no one I knew seemed to be around."

"When you died, were you not met by anyone you knew but by folk you didn't know?"

"Yes."

"I suppose this is possible. Did you find yourself in touch with people you knew?"

"I asked where I was and actually filled my mind with an horrendous fear of kidnapping."

"Did some of the people try to help?"

"I came to realise most of the people I saw spoke about visiting my family later, when I regained myself. They said relatives would find me. Then rotten words left my lips."

"You were somewhat upset?"

"I did not want very many of them to visit. I had had little contact for some time."

"You thought why should they appear after that time. What was the response to that?"

"I said I did not want to see relatives, only my wife."

"I see."

"They said that was not possible. Then I really blew my top!"

"Did they try to soothe you?"

"I reckoned they were wanting to get hold of my money."

"You felt you were alive on Earth in your normal physical body and people round were solid Earth folk?"

"I gave them a bad time. I fumed for days it seemed. Nobody seemed bothered."

"Did they attempt to explain to you what had happened?"

"No, I know I would not have believed them."

"Did someone stay with you, were you in a house?"

"It seemed like a hotel. Comfortable rooms. I was eventually flummoxed at everything seeming relaxed and no-one tried to harm me. I eventually asked who they were, expecting to be told I was their prisoner and must wait till a ransom had been paid!"

"Instead of that what did they tell you?"

"They said they were helpers. Told me I was dead and that was the reason I could not see my wife."

"How did you receive that?"

"I did not believe them. After all, people are burnt when dead so how could I be dead?"

"I can understand your reasoning if you had had no thought about existing in another body!"

"I think they knew I would feel like that. Then someone decided the time had come to meet folk I would recognise, so in came Gran! I knew she was dead. I thought I was dreaming. She sat and talked. She said she would come back another day with other relatives. I just thought I was dreaming! People said it was time I moved and posted a letter home to my wife. I said I would phone her."

"So they encouraged that, to go and look for a telephone."

"I went outside but it seemed foggy, and I didn't know where to go. People seemed only to be former colleagues, but none of them stopped to talk. I was still director."

"So what was the next step?"

"I asked to see the person in charge! I was kindly told that no-one was in charge, so I just felt helpless. I was being treated kindly. No-one wanted payment. I felt lost and kind of powerless. Then gran returned with others I knew were all dead. I was open-mouthed!"

"Did you still think you were dreaming?"

"I somehow knew it was not a dream."

"So that is the tale of how you came to die and start a life in another world you never knew existed."

Polly

22.1.89.

"Before I died I rebelled against religion. I used to think I would make good compost. When I arrived here I found that my assumption was very wrong. I find I am much as before. I have a much more militant approach to disdainful people than I ever had. I feel this is because no one here dispenses anything but love, and it irritates me to see that it is not always appreciated."

"Interesting concept!"

"I find some people make a lot of trouble for others, even here. I think some resent the loss of position. The truth is, no-one here has any privileges that he has not earned."

"What sort of privileges are you speaking about?"

"I mean some people can travel, some can help others, but all must justify themselves first. Nothing is given just for pleasure. I mean senses are used because one has tied together remnants of past lives, and learned from mistakes.

Knowledge brings ability to share with others. Hence, more activities are possible."

George   12.2.89

After identifying himself, George said he had had the experience of coming 'out of his body' in previous illnesses:~

"I came out of my body during my last illness too. I now know it is quite normal to do so when you are near so-called 'death'. It means your spirit is separating from the physical body and is not something to fear. I have found out so much that is exciting. The idea that everybody seems to imagine a terrible end to everything is far from the truth. I assumed I would be finished but life here is fuller and happier than I long ago fancied.

I find so much more peace here. No-one gives out punishment for one's failings. They give loving words of encouragement instead.

I like to think I am prepared to learn. Many mistakes are made in the process. A lot has yet to be found out. I now know that if you ask for help, it is very quickly given. Strange we live so long on earth in complete ignorance! I know it is mostly self-inflicted ignorance. We aim in the wrong direction. We are concerned with intellectual pursuits, or else with amusements and impressing others with our omnipotence.

I just know now that I have endless opportunity for getting to grips with difficulties. I believe I chose the manner of my departure. I am not sure that I achieved what I had hoped. One reviews this, you know. I like to think there were successes as well as failures."

Harry   16.3.89

"I ought to explain why I am here. I have your channel tonight because a lot has happened to me that Peter thought you should know about. Because I made a lot of money on earth, I had a very difficult time when I arrived here."

"Have you been long on your side?"

"Must be about forty years. I made guns then. I won government contracts. I found I was considered to be a go-getter and considered myself to be needed to foster the war effort."

"You thought you counted for something!"

"I personally was too old to be called up."

"Had you owned a factory before the war?"

"No, I was a tool maker."

"You made a lot more money than you could have expected to in your lifetime?"

"It went to my head. When I came here I expected I would be acknowledged as a hero. Important to keep the guns rolling."

"Was this big guns, artillery?"

"Yes, I had great difficulty in losing what I had gained. I had only held a position of power for a brief time but I was shattered to find I no longer counted any more than a good many other people. I fought everybody I encountered, or tried to! You see you cannot achieve anything here that way. I got more and more frustrated because the more I fought the less people I saw to fight! You must realise here we are drawn together by love, and where this does not exist, there is a void. You eventually find yourself alone with your thoughts.

I was sometimes visited by helpers but although they were helpers, they completely dedicated themselves to listening to your moans. Every time despair gripped me, I was sympathetically listened to and asked what I envisaged doing about it! You have no idea how dreadful you feel. I had no question in my mind but that I was a victim of some ghastly criminal gang!"

"Surely they explained in some way?"

"Yes, but without some idea that you survive death, how can you start to understand what is happening? I lived alone for much of the time. I could see other people but seemed not to be forming any friendships. It was a long time before I cottoned-on to the fact that it was all up to me. My message is that everything is possible here once you can use reality for helping others and not for any gain for self."

(See also 16.3.89, *Ways of helping others.*)

Vincent   10.2.89

"I have found life here is all and more than I ever hoped. I have been to lectures. I have noticed much that is beautiful. I feel that for those who have no idea of what to expect, life here metes out different experiences. Some folk seem to sit all day. They do not make use of all the possibilities. One must want to find out more. The extent of possible knowledge is unlimited. I am only touching on how one can spend one's time.

I enjoy meeting those of common interest. Philosophy used to intrigue me. I have found there to be scope for infinite discussion with minds much more developed than I had dreamt of. The love and dedication, and also the patience that the dedicated teachers show is of such magnitude that one feels how small one is! Modesty about one's own small gifts just have to be acknowledged. Sometimes one is in sheer awe at the understanding shown by great minds about the trivia which we spend so much of our lives arguing about.

I must say Peter shows signs already of this type of understanding. He has clearly given much time already to helping other misguided souls. He brings much humour to life. He also sends out a lot of love."

Peter   3.6.89

"Sadly Earth still refers to people's departure instead of to their return home."

"Does everybody on your side feel they have returned home?"

"Not in the same way. Everybody being at different stages have their own needs and for some 'home' will remain Earth, and material things, because they still have not grown beyond such pleasures."

"Several communicators had quoted material things they missed such as pretty clothes, the pub and sex. Why do people not come back quickly to Earth?"

"Not always anxious to have a different life. They want to keep to the familiar, when they need to experience, only have not the courage. Yesterday always seems desirable."

Ways of helping others

Death can be an opportunity for further growth and service to others, not specifically through communication with Earth incarnates, but by help given to fellow discarnates. Hence, many speak of 'rescue work' in various forms, perhaps best described as giving love and understanding to those distressed and puzzled by transition and often in need of temporary hospice-type care.

Bob   2.12.88

Having spoken about the motorcycle accident in which he died many years ago, Bob reported his Rescue work activity:-

"You told us last evening that you were engaged in rescue work. I presume this involves descending to Earth level to Souls unable to let go for some reason or other?"

"Yes, that's right. We get a request from our supervisor, who is continually scanning the appointed area for problems and descend to the particular problem, attempting to persuade the person concerned to let go and come with us back up to the light. We feel like deep-sea divers without a suit and cannot stay too long in the heavy murky depths."

"Are people loth to let go of the Earth level?"

"Yes, quite often. You cannot blame them when it is all they know! They expected to go out like a light on death and are quite mystified at being still alive but unable to attract the attention of people still living. Since they have nothing else in their minds to go on, they cling on to what they know, the Earth. So we have to gently persuade them that there is something better if they come with us. Some are happy to do so. Others are stubborn and abusive. If their reaction is too bad, we just have to leave them to cool off a bit and return later." (See also 7.3.89, *Problem of communicating*).

Ropo   2.3.89

"I want to tell you about my attempt to get to help a new arrival. I found her wandering in the dark. I evidently surprised her by speaking."

"She was lost and alone? Had she only just arrived?"

"She had been here a short time but she had not met anybody."

"Ropo, when people pass over, we thought there was always someone who met them. Is this not so?"

"No one has to meet a relative and if the person is not very advanced she would not be in the mind of an advanced teacher, so no one would automatically be detailed that way. I know many people are observed just as they arrive but others can slip through unnoticed."

"Then some people get stuck and don't make it to your side?"

"I think unless they are very troubled souls they do get to the outskirts of the so-called Summerland."

"Is this where you saw this person wandering in the dark?"

"Yes. I made myself known to her and asked her to follow me. I took her to a group of helpers and now she is being cared for. She should have been met by relatives, only they argued among themselves and so no-one was there at the moment of departure from Earth."

Phyllis   2.3.89

"I am very busy and very happy. I work in a hospital for mentally disturbed people. I attempt to help them recover their normality. I find them very confused and still trying to do much as they did on Earth. I have to get them to relax and sleep."

"How do you achieve that degree of relaxation?"

"I have people with me who can transmute healing energies, and these suffuse the entire aura. A question of changing the vibrations and then they sample love for the first time. I find my attempts to talk to them must wait till they have absorbed most of the energies they need."

"Is this experience (of mental handicap) on Earth taken on only by advanced Souls?"

"I think so. It is a tremendous handicap on Earth and I doubt a lot of less advanced souls could entertain the idea. Most of them have attempted to get a picture of man's inhumanity. I find it very demanding. I also feel I add something to their understanding of the experience by being able to talk about good that some on Earth are trying to do for them."

"Do the people on your side not see Earth therapies as helpful?"

"I think the outstanding comment is that 'they felt no love'"

165

Harry   16.3.89

"I am doing rescue work now and finding that it is giving me happiness. The message is that it is a long haul and your lack of everything is due to your inability to have the right thoughts."

"Any idea how long it took you to have the necessary step forward?"

"I think many years. A great deal depends on love of one's fellow men. I don't think I had ever given thought to that. I have a lot of work to do connected with my application to reincarnate. I feel I need to progress and now feel I have taken a step forward, so I want to try again. I need to show I can conquer selfishness."

"That's one of the basic human characteristics to take in hand. In Rescue Work you are truly helping others. Then you wish to incarnate? Wish you the best of luck! You will be coming to Earth at a hard time."

"I believe the main thing is to try. I have wasted time on totally despicable pride."

"Being quite tough on yourself now."

"I am glad to have spoken."

The problem of communicating with Earth folk

Bill   23.2.89

"I had no idea I would be in such a delightful place."

"Would you like to tell us what you found.?"

"I was met by good friends."

"People you knew?"

"Yes I recognised a friend from war years."

"Were you both in the forces together?"

"Yes."

"Was he killed during the war?"

"Yes."

"That must have been a surprise."

"I know I immediately realised I had died. I had just thought I was hallucinating. He gathered me up and took me to a large house. I not only was welcome, I was put to bed and told to sleep as long as I liked. I must have been particularly tired because I dropped off straight away. I must have been there some time. I missed my family and asked if I could see them. I was told yes, but they will not know you are there. I decided I must take a look. So, lots of colleagues came too, and we drifted into the beneficial state of mind. I then thought about everyone I loved and found I was 'a fly on the wall' in my old home. Found my wife was happy and making plans to move and live near my son. I am sure she will get on very well and make a life for herself. Don't think she had any idea I was there."

Robert 7.3.89

"I must begin by attempting to give a picture of life here. I arrived some time ago from a body that had been badly knocked around. I arrived here very depleted emotionally and lost. As I had no friends here I panicked when I had no need.

I found myself sitting in a beautiful garden. On first seeing this I knew I was dead because I had read about the beauty of heaven. I had never considered that I should be able to see other people and talk to them.

I became disturbed when I knew nobody there. A Being of light made me more anxious. Everybody was very kind but I felt overawed. Love was evident everywhere but I couldn't understand why I should be given this. I felt some trick must be involved.

I asked for my family and was told I could visit them later. The Being of light said someone loved me very much and might sense my presence. I cannot recall anyone in my family ever saying they had been aware of relatives who had died.

I decided to visit my home. No-one seemed aware I called. I made efforts to give my ailing mother a hug but made no impact. I called mother because I could sense her despair although she knew I had departed in many ways after the accident. I do wish she could see me now."

"You have none of your problem left by the accident I presume?"

"I am not disabled at all now. I enjoy a good many things and have accepted my demise from Earth. I just wish I could talk to my family again. I know they believe I am alive in spirit, but they have no idea that some of us are keen to keep contact and be included still.

Alternatively, I am trying to say families exclude knowledge of discarnates from everyday talk. We, if interested, are aware yet are not considered anymore. I wish everybody became knowledgeable once a loved one died."

Thomas
30.4.89

"I know I am here. You now know I am an individual talking with you. You cannot know I was called Thomas when last on Earth because you never met me. You have no means of identifying me, whereas with Peter you brought him up from childhood knowing all his idiosyncrasies, expressions, and illgotten gains, as well as his moments of anguish. So to you, his expressions, his use of long words, his love and concern, become obvious to you, yet coming from an unseen source.

Please remember he is only unseen because as yet you have been unable to raise your vibrations to match his present ones. I see him very clearly as a big, smiling, golden-haired man, who oozes concern for others. He has infinite patience with difficult people, that is by my standards. He is often less than satisfied. He decided to give a great commitment to establishing his continued existence and, I think, deserves to get some Earthly recognition for his efforts. I know nothing could happen without your commitment, but for the moment I am going to accept that as deserved. Peter told me how he has tried to establish not only his identity, but the fact of reincarnation.

It appears that you have finally given total acceptance to his continued existence. I know you have battled with doubts. I hope you are now beyond doubting. I do, however, realise that others doubt the entire experience. For you this must be continually a source of frustration, and sometimes must recreate sadness in your lives. I know Peter is most concerned that this should not happen.

I have discovered that so many people here lose interest completely in Earth, and their connections become like a closed book. After all, life always seems sweeter when knowledge is more complete, and for most people here death was feared. So now they feel relieved. Some question 'What next?' Others do not care to wonder, just like to exist.

If one questions the future one needs to act, and for most of us much work remains. I am referring to our characteristics which leave much to be desired very often. But one is supported here in one's efforts. I therefore think so much effort is worthwhile.

I can only respond by trying to assist Peter's attempt to 'prove' reincarnation is automatic, if you want to learn self-control. So far little effort has been put into establishing this."

One's character is an open book

A Dutchman   12.3.89

"I have difficulty in realising that my thoughts are accessible to everyone. Failure to control these can cause a lot of embarrassment. Not everybody is prepared to send out love when you are critical of them."

"Are there many clashes engendered by that?"

"Yes! I have much to learn. Don't believe many people are a lot different from Earth, just no longer able to hide behind false smiles."

"To what degree is there conversation between different people?"

"I think speech is used for constructive purposes. People discuss different understanding of life, and many go to classes for this purpose. Less idle gossip than on Earth."

Review of previous incarnations

The review of one's life can give rise to regret and distress. One sees the reason one failed in handling a situation and the effect on others. But, as is shown by Peter in chapter 9 *A Record of Past Lives*, and in others examples, understanding gives rise to a determination to resolve character traits and to progress spiritually.

Ken   30.8.88

Charles Kenneth Pizzey (Ken), died in 1958, a cousin of June Cowlin in his last life:~

"I know Peter is deeply aware of the purpose in his recent life. I wish I could see half as clearly as Peter why I did reincarnate as Charles Kenneth Pizzey.

I tried to add more time to my last life by avoiding direct contact with illness. Tried to avoid meeting people who were ill. Yet I was forced to face (his wife) Connie's illness."

"That was very distressing for you."

"I drank too heavily once I knew she had cancer. I used to pray that the growth would not kill her."

"Clearly a traumatic period."

"I wish now I had sat up late, instead of going to bed when she was so ill. I used to run away from the problem. I have talked about this with wiser people. They told me I would have another chance to do a similar thing. One has got to prove oneself. I know I tried to cope then but failed. I know I must give more time to others in my next life."

5.8.89

We noted that Ken had recalled several earlier lives, indicating connections with Peter and supporting the idea of 'group incarnation'. Ken summarises his experience:~

"I want to give a summary. I see you have got three lives."

"Got Ken, Tom, someone who made candles, and maybe a fourth. Yes, Memstec's sister's husband. That makes four lives."

"I forgot the life as a slave. I realise that throughout, my behaviour has been governed by the need to be admired. I know now that it is a question of trying to give out love unselfishly. Not giving for reward. Love is the basis on which God's plan is designed but He never demands anything in return. I find I have not mastered this, only tried in the life as your cousin.

I had for the previous four incarnations always put myself first. I also was not completely confident in my ability to cope alone. I therefore always tried to overcome this by incarnating with a strong-minded wife in mind. However, this in itself is not an answer. Try asserting yourself when someone is determined to overrule any fresh idea! I think in putting big hopes in one basket I was really trying to do too much at once.

Probably, I was misguided by my own need for boosting my deflated ego. I consequently seem to have been in need of artificial support in the past four lives. Question is whether I am about to make the right decisions about future incarnations. I have almost left it too late. Tend to think I have got to have great faith in my own ability to be my own man throughout. Not sure I can do this without decidedly strong support. This means emotional compassion, not selfish aim.

Unless I get this, I shall have to battle again to resist the easy way out, namely alcohol or stimulant of some sort. These as you know present yet a further demeaning of spirit and can be the downfall of a lot of otherwise loveable doting family men, or even women.

I have been lacking, most of all, unconditional love. Good intentions have therefore eluded me. Mastery of desire for image is terribly difficult in any case, and I seem to have been unable to do without props. I have got to make a very careful judgement. I realise the environment in which I grow up can settle at an early stage my confidence in myself being handled. I then have to give thought to emanating the role of capable manager in home situation. I think I have got to look for someone who can encourage me rather than decide for me. I just wish I had not let so many basic characteristics go unacknowledged so long."

"Well, may you not have a few more strengths you can link in with from earlier lives?"

"Yes."

"Other thing that comes to mind: is there any possibility of you being a woman next time round?"

"I think emotionally an equal role will be played by both sexes in the future of individual development. The Woman's role in society may place more decision-making on her, so I doubt I can escape that way!

I have, I am told, taken a big step forward in acknowledging my needs. I now have to plan without anticipating any easy option. Peter is actually giving lots of encouragement, and I see the need to be positive, not dwelling on failure, but trying to build-in realistic aims appears to be the name of the game."

"Sounds an incredibly difficult operation from here."

"I think we belong to a spiritual group which has been struggling together for aeons of time. One can branch out, but that would be unwise. Evidence shows much love is available for group members. Sadly I still need love and support given, but intend to keep up, and finally repay support with interest!"

7.8.89

Ken adds more insight into the life experienced as an American slave:~

"I have looked again at the records and particularly at the life I had momentarily forgotten, the one in South Carolina. Can see why I chose to quickly forget!

The good thing about it was entirely an opportunity to experience Man's inhumanity to his brethren. The fear it engendered in me completely overwhelms me. Lust and cruelty was the mark of the whiteskin, and subservience and broken hearts were the lot of black-skinned man.

Rebecca and I loved each other deeply, but seldom were able to express this in anything other than a brief physical encounter. I was totally incapable of protecting her from indecent assault, and my heart and spirit were greatly denigrated by this experience, to such a degree that I have resorted to a less protective role in later relationships. I see a lot of damage was done to my ego in that life, and has resulted in problems in making confident relationships. Evidence still remains. Some positive steps must be taken to redress the balance. I feel I have failed miserably in re-establishing a personal model of a confident spirit.

Hence, as I said recently, I still find difficulty in acting entirely on my own decisions. At least now I shall go ahead understanding why I have this problem unresolved. I see why so much karma has been acquired by some who, in the past, have retaliated against violence with yet more inhumanity. This I know is not the way forward.

One must learn to advance in spirit by use of love, not force. Whatever the depreciation of ego, one must keep one's values. Integrity is much prized here. I see one must carry a banner in one's mind that has on it,

'Remember love, for the entire creation of God is the goal.' I must go now."

Nona   26.6.88

Nona, June's mother, died in 1985. We were told by several communicators that Nona was having great difficulty in coming to terms with reincarnation. She had disliked the concept when on Earth, she felt it implied she would not meet old friends. Following Peter's revelation that he had previously incarnated as Charles (her father), she became deeply depressed, and we were eventually told that specialist help had been sought for her to assist her face the concept:~

"I go to classes about reincarnation. Got eventually to know what I achieved in my last life. Sometime have to decide my future arrival. I am not anxious to be born again. I know people won't acknowledge reincarnation. No good denying."

                                                    28.8.88

Eventually Nona gave information about her earlier life. The experience of re-appraisal caused considerable distress:~

"I know now that I used to live in the USA. I was Ropo's mother."

"Did you always live in America?"

"No, I actually came from Italy."

"Who were you married to?"

"I believe he used to sail to USA."

"As a passenger?"

"No."

"Crew of a boat?"

"He was a captain, involved in the slave trade. I realise many people tried Rome as an umbrella for dirty work."

"How did you come to be in America?"

"I must look again."

"Anything else about this?"

"I was dismayed about the whole thing."

29.1 89

"A lot of God's plan is degraded by human frailties. I had no idea death was like this. I just find it difficult to accept that people I have known well and loved can have been responsible for some of the misery that one has heard about."

"Do see everyone on a path trying to advance."

"No, I cannot go forward alone."

A near state of panic seemed to follow, which one tried to calm with positive suggestion.

26.4.89

Peter, bringing Nona forward to communicate:~

"I have brought Nona with me. I would like to say a word about the demanding situation which she is facing. She must come to terms with her past and this she finds difficult."

"Yes, understand that."

"Here she is. Nona is here."

"Long time since we heard from you."

Nona:~

"I have not been well. I have been upset, I felt I must talk."

"Last time you talked you said you would tell us something about your last life."

"I have been looking at my past."

"Everyone does eventually."

173

"Not everyone bothers to look beyond their recent life. Sometimes they forget their recent life as soon as possible."

"That's not very constructive."

"I sometimes wish I had not looked. I was linked up with a lot of people involved in the slave trade."

"You told us that once before."

"I went to America often on a boat taking slaves."

"A lot of people must have done that. A good way of getting experiences. What year was it?"

"I think 1805 I died. I lived in Italy in the 1700's and early 1800's anyway."

"What age were you when you died?"

"I was about 40. A long life was unusual in those days, but pregnancy was common late in life by your standards. I see that I did nothing to stop the cruelty. Considering the stench on the boat, I am amazed that I went. I used to be the only white woman on board"

She had loathed smells in her previous life. She went on to give a horrendous description of life on the boat and the part she had played:~

"I have so much karma, I hardly know where to begin."

"There must be a lot of people in the same situation from that period of time."

"I realise that I have to reincarnate to begin to handle things differently. I used to think once you got here you could have some peace from the worries of earth. I now see that I have been under a false impression.

I feel I should try to help Earth folk understand what life is for. So yes, talk about my existence. Do not feel you are giving away a confidence. All information given must be used to help Earth folk understand."

"Yes, people are still so blind, they do not realise what they do now will have affected Earth when they return. So we want to be able to describe your good and bad experiences. Sure you must look back further to try and find these threads, and decide which characteristics you have to cope with and how. Decide on some things you can cope with successfully to boost your morale."

"Evidently you don't think too badly of me."

"It is not a question of feeling good about people who are doing wonderful things and bad about people who are doing wrong things. There are things

we all need to learn as they are doing. So I find it fascinating to look back on your reactions in your last life."

Peter   27.4.89

"I want first to say how consoled Nona was after speaking to you."

"We are delighted to know that. Part of her life seems to have been horrendous. I wonder if there was a very different aspect to that life?"

"I feel it was indeed a black life. She must accept it and rediscover her true self. I feel there is a big debt to repay and she must initially get to grips with herself; accept her role in that dreadful demeanour of souls. I grieve for her distress. I shall try to help her through the next phase. I know there is a lot that is positive desiring to manifest.

The important thing is to find belief in oneself and understand what is happening in the process of birth and so-called death."

"Obviously one has to comprehend and accept the process to get very far."

"I feel she has accepted what happened but not the heavy responsibility that inevitably occurs. This is where confidence in one's own inner core is of vital importance. A good deal of work on that score remains for Nona to do."

"That makes sense. Wonder whether a lot of that inner strength is hidden with her higher self?"

"It may be but I feel it was abandoned some time ago, and therefore your process of reuniting is not easy. I have said before that considerable one-mindedness is essential. The program for recall is not given you on a plate. One has to be strong minded about seeking it out. It can be very irksome, and encouragement is appreciated along the line, though you yourself have to stay with it. A small step forward that gives a hint of light is worth a great deal.

I must try to see Nona begs for some more insight. Someone, Petrach[1] perhaps, might then call on her, and compassion has a big part to play in the appropriate formulation of intention."

"I get the idea, cement the determination to go forward."

29.4.89

Nona completes her review:~

"I have given much thought to our conversation about my past life. I realise I am erring in trying to forget the past, and have decided to start going to classes to try my hand at understanding why I did what I did."

1   See *Appendix of Names.*

"That sounds an excellent idea! Very positive and constructive. Might be quite fascinating."

"I know I have to keep on learning otherwise I shall get left behind when you all do other things. I find it humiliating to realise I have been so unkind to many in the past but receive nothing but kindness here."

"This is something you will also be able to give!"

"I have got to try to understand myself before I can be of much help to others."

"This decision is a big step in the right direction."

"I have been so depressed, no one stayed long with me, but I find already that is changing."

"A good deal faster than on Earth!"

"I have even been to see Ropo myself today. He was so kind I felt I must go."

"That was an excellent idea."

"He is moving to a big house where he can take visitors needing recuperation and says I can live there."

"Could you go to your classes from there?"

"Yes, I might be able to help some of them by talking about the classes."

"Sounds excellent. Do you like the idea?"

"Yes, I have been alone too long."

Asked why the trauma did not occur earlier concerning the life described:~

"I find you forget. I have yet to understand a lot about my acceptance of life's lessons. I believe that until one accepts the disapproval internally, one is left with all the trauma unresolved. I just wanted to tell you about my decision."

"Thank you."

Coco   4.2.90

Coco, June's father, died in 1981:~

"Just want to say I am making good progress, and shall come back another time to tell you a lot of details. I have found out a lot of things that are very important. You are likely to be shocked by what I tell you, but it indicates the way things are.

Because we all must climb a ladder, we fall off sometimes and in doing so take steps forward afterwards. I am now considering my next step. I hoard much past karma, as do so many, but sadly last time round I failed to handle what I needed to do. A question of making a wrong decision early on. I must sort out my mistakes so that I can give you an idea of how we get our priorities, I mean the thoughts behind our actions.

We are not very open with each other on earth. Here only truth is seen, whether it is nice or murky. It makes things easier really. A lot of forgiveness is required on all sides. Some hide away after initial shock and revel in the beauty of our surroundings. This one needs to do at times but there's no point in sitting around indefinitely.

Once one has acknowledged one's failures nothing is gained by this, one has no need to look back. Once one has accepted the situation, one must act. When one does that, love alone surrounds one.

Normally there's no gloom here. I've realised how often I said 'cheer up' to folk on earth. No long faces once positive thoughts are established here. An opportunity both for making lots of knowledgeable friends and letting past mistakes sleep. Also to learn so much fresh information about the universe. A fresh opportunity is always there.

I soon learned I must forgive others their mistakes. Another step was to forgive myself! Once a question of regret becomes positive thought for the future, the world is your oyster. I do not mean Earth, perhaps I should have said, 'The universe is the stage for all to use'. The only requirement being good intentions.

A lot of mistakes are made. This is of no account other than as a stepping stone. So, struggle on ducks! I am very happy to talk again."

Ropo   21.2.89

An early Victorian relative. Looking more closely at the Akashic Records and trying to understand his last life he said:~

"I will have to return to Earth at some time. I don't like the idea, I must learn to take more lenient a view of young people. I now know I must try to help them more."

"Well, attitudes have changed as regards parental responsibilities."

"I must say I just hope I can improve my control of my temper. I need to improve very much my way of handling children. Hope I have another opportunity to try."

"Is it difficult to get opportunities to try Ropo?"

"It depends on whether I really make our helpers believe that I have a positive approach to my failings."

"You almost have to have permission?"

"I think you need backing."

"Seems from here an immense task to sort out what is needed and where to find it."

"I sometimes think I must make more effort to establish a better link with other groups."

"Have more discussion on different things you mean? You were trying to sort out your religious beliefs at one time."

"I then wanted to satisfy myself that I had not dreamt up the teachings I had experienced on Earth."

"Concerning religion?"

"Yes, I found everything so different. I still fail to understand why we all are so ignorant on Earth. I feel when I next incarnate, I may be able to bring down some positive attributes, and Peter assures me that having acknowledged my weaknesses, they begin to become my strengths."

Summary – Linking lives with groups   19.10.89

Peter reviews the relationships that can be maintained in group incarnation, and states the task we face as individuals:~

"I have to comment on the foregoing attempts to establish our survival of death. I have spoken of our links with other lives and how we entwine our experiences with other folk, usually for a specific purpose.

Frequently we live our lives with various spirits that we have known before. With some, we shall have had a very close and purposeful relationship. With others, we shall have rubbed shoulders in the course of life's experiences. The remaining group may also belong to our specific spiritual family but still be on the lower slopes of the mountain. So we can be directly affecting others in their experiences, or just giving support along the way.

If you will but briefly consider my words and now re-read the words of these other communicators I feel perhaps that you are more likely to accept that they have all tried to make a contribution in their own light of actual experience to the understanding of the World once one no longer inhabits a physical body.

I shall now try to explain why each must focus on personal experience, and how eventually that experience is actually differently perceived. I must make myself reasonably clear by stressing that no one is forced to stand alone after arrival here. The decision is entirely his own. The ability to move on and expand one's knowledge is entirely thought-based.

If you are content to sit recalling past joys and not questioning the possibility of alternative ways of thinking; if you are anxious not to lose worldly prestige; if you have misgivings about forgetting past experiences that caused aggravation, you can continue with those thoughts but may not find yourself welcome company for those who once shared those degrading lifestyles. They may have acknowledged the use of the happenings of a past life and moved on in thought and vision."

Giving thought to changing priorities   31.3.89

Peter concludes that a change of priorities is urgently required:~

"I said once before how impossible it is to be of help, unless Earth folk decide we have a part to play in Earthly matters. We give much thought to the focus of your lives when we are concerned for your welfare; I mean, when we feel a strong bond, which generally means we are part of the same spiritual group. But, we can only put in a supply of love and hopefully inspire in a subtle way. We cannot decide how anyone acts and so often the personality comes tumbling over the inspiration.

The personality is often thought to be of greater consequence because man generally still thinks his intellectual decision is more valid than his intuition, or the thought inspired by his higher self mixed in with our effort to influence. While we on Earth attach so much importance to self, as most of us did before we came here, and could see more clearly, this will remain a totally discriminatory business, and open to abuse, as some will give credence to higher sources of influence without justification and others will fail to act on constructive guidance. So be it!

Sadly, time is running out. As I have said before, Mankind can destroy Earth and have to reincarnate elsewhere if he wishes to experience other difficulties. However, the possibilities will be less amenable for many. I am trying to say that some would be limited by virtue of the stage of development they have reached.

I know it is very important to change Earth priorities quickly. Please do not think it does not matter. The outcome is still not fixed, but it is inevitable unless change in lifestyles is made, and is made soon. I can no longer think in Earth years, but surely it should be enough to realise time is short, or is Mankind unable to care about future generations?

Even if he has not accepted reincarnation, he does at least accept the general principle of Man's ability to produce off-spring. He needs to give some thought to their need for natural resources, as well as electronic wizardry."

11. Reason for Life on Earth

A call for beauty, Deciding priorities – a charitable approach,
Eternal Man, Freedom from 'good intentions', In pursuit of learning,
Let nature take it's course, God's vision – a summary.

In this final chapter, Peter makes a call for an appraisal of personal
values, and concludes, in his summary, with the reasons for Man
living Earth lives:~

A call for beauty   15.3.89

"I mostly want to give time to a construction of concepts that are
appropriate to your everyday life:

I have a commitment to helping as many people as possible to
grasp the reality of Eternity. I want you to construct a beautiful,
warm vision of everybody living as one... the lost community spirit
being the concept I am trying to put across.

Visualise the existence of beauty undiminished by aggression,
hate, envy, selfishness and grief. There is no other reason for these
things except greed. This is the basis of trouble in the world at the
present time. It is essential that people acknowledge that there is no
good reason to covet possessions. In this world a host of beautiful
things are available to those who open their hearts to love.

A decision that can only be made by an individual soul, the ability
to contain behaviour within that required for development of spirit,
is the reason for life on Earth. Were we meant to succeed while
others failed, some would be devoid of frailties. This is not so. All
men have an equal chance to lift themselves from the despicable
manner of spiritual debasement.

Not everyone has struggled the same amount of time. As you have
noted from communications some have been content to be here for
long periods, for centuries in fact. The trouble is, time is no longer
of no consequence. Planet Earth is in real trouble and cannot

survive indefinitely without drastic changes in people's way of thinking. So desperate change is needed."

Deciding priorities – a charitable approach   10.6.89

"I am often still amazed, I question whether a lot of people understand what charity is really about. In the dictionary I hope it will give a broader meaning than the usual use. It implies a sincerity that is sadly lacking in the world and is a definite bonus as far as character is concerned. I rarely see it as Mankind bustles around doing what he calls 'big business'."

"Don't suppose there is too much to be seen!"

"I think perhaps most are trying to understand behaviour concerning their relationships and hopefully will eventually discover how it was they failed when so many necessary ingredients were on hand. Wasted opportunities are so very obvious from here, one wonders why the whole thing was not appreciated as an *opening for giving*, rather than allowed to slip into a decidedly less fruitful occasion."

"Sure we all miss opportunities, for selfish reasons probably."

"Deciding priorities is the stumbling block. Too frequently the wrong decision is made. I generally observe a holiday atmosphere about taking decisions, though sometimes a sense of duty to a different cause is indicated.

Acquiring a right balance is something else to learn. I feel a lot could be done by giving a very small amount of time to another, perhaps voluntary cause.

I abhor the use of a life in which so much effort is directed apparently to a becoming image. I refer to being an accepted 'pillar of society' with all the irrelevant excesses. Please do not think I am being critical, I am just observing things that will give cause for regret on your return home. A little more effort could have been the means of closing another otherwise uncompleted valuable lesson in character. A lot of such behaviour wastes your time on Earth.

I believe something drastic will need to happen before much interest is taken in the basic truth underlying reality. I sadly see such a lack of interest common to so many people who could make progress this time round. I speak of important progress, because Earth folk are on a decidedly slippery surface.

I must agree that it is unfortunate that we invest so much effort in so-called intellectual pursuits. A lot of real learning is accomplished best through other activities. It is only when an actual career is needed for a specific activity that such a degree of 'book' learning is required. Usually one would then know the importance of the effort. Those who drift do not align themselves with their soul's requirements.

Do not think I considered how closed people's minds are to such concepts. Strange how long it takes to know that one really has a permanent home here. I suppose it is linked to the amount of experience which needs to be acquired once one accepts the situation. I think some problems are no longer valid."

"The acquisition of material wealth enables people to do things they wouldn't have done 50 years ago. People go to University partially for social life. Surely this cannot be entirely negative for the outcome!"

"Negative if they do not then utilise a situation for what it can open up. Social relationships cannot be avoided, so opportunities appear whatever course is followed."

Eternal Man   15.6.89

"I think if Man could accept that he is involved in long term experience he would not put so much effort into eliminating all possible sources of experience. A moderate improvement of a natural environment would keep people in good shape and leave opportunity for short lives as necessary.

I would point out that many infectious illnesses have not just been controlled, but virtually have no chance of being the means by which spirits can gain quick return here. Other ways have to be found for the purpose of giving the experience of loss to many who have to try to come to terms with their own needs. It postpones the knowledge of the question of survival too. The death of anyone by insidious disease striking out from no inner recognised source gives much food for thought. It has become increasingly difficult for young children to depart. Leukaemia is a current possibility and hence is apparently prevalent in the western world."

"Mankind doesn't see things in this light. It is incredibly hard on parents."

"I think sometimes no thought is given to what experience means."

"People don't look on the Earth world to such experience that is positive. It is not seen as a plan, and doesn't come into the thinking of authorities who are responsible for health."

"Now, such questions should be filtered through. Concern is now needed about Eternity and part of this is inevitably linked to Man accepting he must work with nature and accepting that he is not in control and will always be subject to natural forces. He needs to become a partner, not a director."

Freedom from 'good intentions'   23.6.89

"I feel I am nearly at the point of absorbing a comprehensive picture of what I achieved last time round. I should like the final summary to be concise and leave the impression that struggle on Earth with a variety of conflicting streams of interests undoubtedly challenges the physical mind.

I feel that sometimes you need desperately the added impetuous of spiritual uplift. Unfortunately, on Earth at present too much dependency is placed on Man's intellectual powers rather than intuition. One has to be sometimes what is called 'bloody minded' to stick with one's own plan for the life.

Far too much emphasis is being placed on society's comprehension of how one should live. It then becomes very difficult to attempt pragmatic mistakes. One actually becomes a robot instead of freely living what one knows needs to be experienced.

One is constantly trying to battle against a good intentioned service in which other people are assuming that none of your troubles should be allowed to affect you. I only know that people must make their own decisions."

"When trouble descends, young people need a helping hand."

"I can see the problem. The thing is, many of them, I believe, have run away from the problem that they intended to handle, and of course a lot of other problems have assumed prior importance: problems for which they can blame society, when in fact they intended to handle emotional problems within a relationship."

"You have a point. It could be!"

"A fresh heart-searching might provide insight, but looking within for some is an uncomfortable occupation. I think you do realise how important it is. I just feel it is not popular in a society which assumes a considerable degree of responsibility for social matters.

"I suppose this has grown to such an extent that the deprivations that accompany a person's experience are deemed unacceptable. I am trying to think how this applies."

"It applies to all we do. I think you had better give time to sorting out this in relation to different situations. People not only must make mistakes, they need to be involved in sorting out the aftermath.

I am not saying help is not needed or should not be given, but it should never be assumed that society has a dictate that can be a panacea for all ills. I am making an attempt to influence your response to other people's outpouring of complaints. Do not let imaginary woes depress you, have faith. An effort to console is useless, as you are aware.

A practical approach is to give out love, and make positive suggestions for change, not unrealistic ones.

Much destruction of society is happening all round the world. It's not possible for heaven to suddenly grow... a lot of destruction of invalid ideas must happen first."

14.7.89

Concerning the problem of 'intellectual education' and the national curriculum:~

"I regard the program as retrograde, I see costly consequences. Intellectual abilities will be of little use to the majority, and the development of practical skills will require a dexterity of hand and eye, not an ability to speak and write standardised English!

I only hope some parents will utilise more time to involve their off-spring in skills that will give scope for innovation. The lack of opportunity will not stop this, but the lack of determination may!

I feel it is an important question of inspiring an idea of achieving independence. I think those who arrive with imagination about independence will probably find scope for its use in plenty of ways. So actually life in the future could offer a lot of inner development, and therefore could be desired by individuals seeking to clinch certain personality characteristics that have not been completely mastered."

Let nature take its course   22.2.90

"Concerning the question of interfering with embryos. Man has got his priorities wrong. Like most things I can see a positive and a negative side to his research."

"The positive side is fertilising eggs which otherwise would not continue to grow."

"Yes, let him do this with love, and the desire to help others; I feel no karma is involved for those who have nothing but these motives in mind.

However the reasons for so desperately needing off-spring should be considered. If it were to give others the chance to experience, then indeed I feel the motive is good. Like many things however, the decidedly difficult procedure is often mostly undertaken for the wrong reasons. It then may result in experience for another spirit, but this means a *loss of original purpose* by the parent. In many cases it provides needed experience of a different kind.

So often the only purpose of research is to try to give everyone a perfect baby. Knowing that fresh experiences are required by all spirits might help people to see that in depriving the child of difficulties, karma is acquired, because far from helping that spirit, only frustration is given. Progress is, in fact, denied.

The handicap of a physical nature is one way of rapidly overcoming inherent difficulties of personality. Done successfully a big step forward is made, not only by the individual afflicted, but by those who give love and care for the spirit along the way. To avoid the experience deliberately, is seen on return here to have been a dastardly decision. Instead of knowing one has handled fresh experience well, one is faced with an extra quantity of karma caused by the rejection of a friend considered well worth while helping from this side of life.

Remember, all babies have chosen their parents, and have tried to plan a life for their progress. Knowing that one has been thwarted and rejected is a cause for much chagrin here. People must try to understand that little is learned from a so called 'good life', compared with one which raises all kinds of emotions and problems. Steps forward are made by successfully endeavouring to place love and caring before pleasure, and like rich people who throw away opportunities for giving care in thought and deed to others, handicapped people can lose much in not attempting to achieve under deliberately engineered circumstances.

Man does not create, he mutates. The creation of all things is God's prerogative. His workers are elementals called Devas. They are important friends of Man. If he only knew it, they would assist him up the mountain. Be not mistaken, they work endlessly for good; without them, Man becomes nothing.

186

They are finding only obstacles put in their way, destroying work done from time immemorial. Can Man wonder that they are complaining now?

A knowledge of home in Eternity might stop man in his tracks. But he is sadly lacking in humility at the present time.

I realise the difficulty in spreading this knowledge. I leave it to you to try. It's a question of time running out."

Summary   12.10.89

"I very often justified my ideas about 'making hay while the sun shone' by questioning whether the real purpose of living was to follow a routine education. I tried to make life work for me, not me to slave for life.

Great store is set by a good many people on achieving maximum knowledge of the past in terms of history, of Nature, in terms of World development, of language as a means of expression and of Science. In comprehension of national progress materially, I have to say that in the rush to fill minds with much that is Man's supposition, good opportunities for reaching truth are missed.

Life on Earth is but a short interlude in our spiritual progress towards determining our final home in eternal communication with God. I therefore want to summarise our reasons for living Earth lives:

A Spirit starts out as a small spark of God's energy. In reality each spark holds the total comprehension of the ultimate truth of Eternity. It exists in God's vision, but *must learn to sustain itself independently.* Earth is the kindergarten to which all have the possibility of entrance. Entrance is not obligatory, never-the-less essential if full independence is to be achieved.

If one is to become an individual entity, having embarked on the initial commitment, there is no other course open. One has become a Spirit, and must attempt to refine one's attributes in order to once again live in God's light. The process demands appraisal of one's whole being.

The objective is to acquire unconditional love for the sanctity of God's creation. Remember, it is His energy that has created the Universe. On Earth, there are numerous examples of His power. As you drive your new car across the land mass you call Earth, please stop to solemnly consider how the ground around you developed; how the animals have come to be so numerous in kind; how the flora has grown in variety. I would suggest that whilst Man interferes, and causes mutations, he is unable to create fresh forms.

In giving such a variety, God has made infinite opportunity available to His divine sparks to flourish, and in the process learn subtle control of basic character traits. They are human personality problems to most of you. In fact, they are the basic energy forms of Life itself.

I repeat, 'humility' is the hallmark of spiritual progress. No one possessing it in full bloom would be handicapped by other lesser evils. Love would emanate without expecting anything in return. Selfishness would be foreign to a possessor of true humility. Greed would be of no meaning.

How could such a person be unkind, or even thoughtless in action? Who do you know who can measure up to such an image? You are indeed fortunate if such a person has apparently crossed your path, because it is to struggle with our failings that we come to Earth! Most of us are only a little way along the road, but we are all struggling towards the goal in our individual ways. Only when we are picking up final embellishments may we sometimes shed a little light on our way."

Epilogue

"A good knowledge of other worlds is appropriate at this time in Earth's history. Each Age contains the necessary ingredients for the advancement of Spirit towards unity with God. Each Age gives opportunity for Man to experience fresh ways of handling problems, as well as being given new aspirations.

I must point out that different manifestations of the same basic characteristics occur throughout time. The response is also different. You are developing along the pathway drawn by God, not by Man. Man sinks or swims according to his knowledge, not of facts, but of God's unerring love.

Only for mastering life's difficulties is 'grace' given. Grace is the Earthly word for ultimate union with a love that knows no bounds.

In his path lie many hazards. It is the attempt to show how the road deteriorates for all of us, but is always rebuilt, and that apparent pits are not bottomless, that has been the object of my attempts at writing a book. I know that my words will be accorded a great deal of scepticism.

But the century ahead will invalidate much contention now, a reason for this being that the Age of Communication is about to dictate certain changes in Man's perception. Not only will he accept the concept, but unless he falls short of his remembering of past lives, he will accord considerable value to the link with those of us out of body, who are able to see more clearly.

I have said before that in the course of our development, humility is the key to progress. We are here keen to guide with both foresight, and in the light of hindsight, not to dictate policy. Man has for ever free will, but the possibility for treading the path with a helping hand out-stretched in love, and often with a twinkle in the all-seeing eye, is there to be grasped; but only if man hastens to obey his mind to consider things beyond his Earthly existence."

"May light be given to you all, and may you be open to observe its usual spread of different colours. No path will appear identical to the one your neighbour treads, but they all lead to God."

The End

THE GREAT INVOCATION

From the point of Light within the Mind of God
Let light stream forth into the minds of men.
Let Light descend on Earth.

From the point of Love within the Heart of God
Let love stream forth into the hearts of men.
May Christ return to Earth.

From the centre where the Will of God is known
Let purpose guide the little wills of men –
The purpose which the Masters know and serve.

From the centre which we call the race of men
Let the Plan of Love and Light work out
And may it seal the door where evil dwells.

Let Light and Love and Power restore the Plan on Earth.

Glossary

AHRIMAN	God of darkness and evil, Zoroastrian religion of Persia.
AKASHIC RECORDS	The imprint on the Spiritual world of all that has ever happened.
ATLANTIS	Lost continent reputedly sunk beneath the Atlantic
BEINGS OF LIGHT	Advanced Spirits.
BOHR	The model of the Atom due to the physicist Niels Bohr.
BULK ERASER	A small electromagnetic device for cleansing magnetic tapes of information.
GUIDE	An advanced Spirit who can communicate to or through a specific person having mediumistic abilities.
N.D.E	Near death experience. An experience of another dimension often recognised by people who are known to have clinically brushed with death.
PERMANENT ATOM	A tiny centre of force around which a Being incarnates.
PLAN	Refers to a plan of life purpose apparently made between us before we all reincarnated.
SPIRITUAL HEALING	A process by which the power of God is requested to raise the level of consciousness of a patient. It may result in physical healing.
SUMMERLAND	A spiritual realm of peace and beauty.
WINTERLAND	The spiritual area to which those people go who, are unable by reason of their negative characters to reside in Summerland.

Appendix of Names

HUGH	A guide, (*see* Glossary).
ANNE	Our daughter, A.F.Cowlin.
PAUL BEARD	Author of "Living On", George Allen & Unwin.
MARY	A guide.
PAUL	A friend with mediumistic abilities.
NONA	June Cowlin's mother.
COCO	June Cowlin's father.
CHARLES	Peter's great grandfather, Charles Pizzey. An earlier incarnation of Peter.
FINDHORN	A spiritual community in Scotland.
RIGEL/VEGA	Family cats.
ELLEN	Wife of Charles Pizzey.
ROBERT	Father of Charles Pizzey.
BEN	Related to an acquaintance, (also known as Robert).
ROPO	Grandfather of Charles Pizzey.
KEN	Second cousin of Peter, and brother-in-law to Charles Pizzey when in incarnation as Tom Greene.
CONNIE	Wife to Ken.
PETRACH	A Being of Light, (*see* Glossary).
MOPSY	Our Basset hound.

Recommended Reading

The following list of book titles has been selected with the aim of encouraging the reader to delve further into the wide range of subjects covered by this Guide, to help promote the knowledge of the 'World of Spirit' which is our true home.

Titles are offered on the following subjects:

Evidence for survival of death, Scientific Studies, Discarnate accounts of life after death, Reincarnation, Healing, Natural Energies, General

1. Evidence for survival of death

1.1. Scientific studies

LIFE AFTER LIFE by Dr.Raymond Moody MD, Bantam Books
Accounts by survivors of clinical death of their experiences as they died.

RETURN FROM DEATH by Margot Grey, Arkana. ISBN 1 85063 019 4.
An exploration of the 'near death experience'.

RECOLLECTIONS OF DEATH by M.B. Sabom MD. ISBN 0 552 12053 7. An investigation by an eminent cardiologist into patients accounts of their near death experiences.

LIVING ON by Paul Beard (Ex-President of the College of Psychic Studies). George Allen & Unwin. ISBN 0 04 133009 9.
A presentation of many different accounts of post-mortem experiences, and an examination of the phenomena from an open minded view-point. One of the best studies of its kind.

SURVIVAL by David Lorimer, Routledge & Kegan Paul. ISBN 0 7102 0003 X. Body, Mind and Death in the light of psychic experience. A scholarly but highly readable work.

THE SUPREME ADVENTURE by Dr. Robert Crookall Bsc (Psych.), James Clarke & Co. Ltd. ISBN 0227 67606 8.
An analysis of psychic communications. Personal testimonies of survival of death, brought together by an eminent scientist to form an impressive study.

1.2. Discarnate accounts of life after death

TESTIMONY OF LIGHT by Helen Greaves, Neville Spearman Ltd. ISBN 85435 1647.
A telepathic account of life after death based upon communion between the minds of two friends. A truly beautiful book.

THE AWAKENING LETTERS, edited by Cynthia Sandys and Rosamond Lehman, Neville Spearman Ltd. ISBN 85978 033 3.
The after life experiences of two discarnate daughters of the editors.

BEYOND DEATH by Stanislav and Christina Grof, Thames and Hudson. ISBN 0 500 81019 2.
Concepts of the after life in different cultures. Well illustrated.

ON THE DEATH OF MY SON by Jasper Swain, Turnstone Books. ISBN 0 85500 0287.
Communications describing his life after death from a discarnate son to his father.

LIFE IN THE WORLD UNSEEN by Anthony Borgia, Psychic Press Ltd.
An account of his after life experiences by an ex-Archbishop of Canterbury.

2. Reincarnation

MANY LIFETIMES by Dr Denys Kelsey MB. and Joan Grant.
An account of the way incidents in earlier lives can react upon behaviour and health in the present life by a psychiatrist who uses the fact of reincarnation in his clinical practise. A classic.

MANY MANSIONS by Gina Cerminara, Neville Spearman.
Includes the important 'readings' made by Edgar Cayce concerning other lifetimes.

A FORGOTTEN TRUTH by Dr.D.M.A. Leggett MA. and M.G. Payne MA. ISBN 0 946259 14 3.
The forgotten truth is that of serial existence, reincarnation in its little-understood form. The purpose of this book is to formulate a framework of faith to give purpose and meaning to human life.

THE CATHARS AND REINCARNATION by Dr Arthur Guirdham, Neville Spearman.
An account of how a persecuted religious group, last together in Medieval France, reincarnated together and were able to recognise each other.

THE WHEEL OF REBIRTH by H.K. Challoner, Theosophical Publishing House.
The author relives vital episodes in previous lives through dreams.

3. Healing

A GUIDE TO SPIRITUAL HEALING by Harry Edwards, The Healer Pub. Co. Ltd.
Offers guidance to the development of Healing abilities.

SO YOU WANT TO BE A HEALER by Don Copland, H. Doust Art & Advert. Ltd., Gillingham, Kent, or Nat. Fed. of Spiritual Healers, Old Manor Farm Studio, Sunbury-on-Thames, Middx.
A booklet that sets out to help beginners interested in becoming Healers.

THE POWER TO HEAL by David Harvey, The Aquarian Press. ISBN 085030 326 5.
An investigation of Healing and the Healing experience.

THE SEVEN LEVELS OF HEALING by Lilla Bek & Philippa Pullar, Rider. ISBN 0 7126 9473 0.
This book provides knowledge of the energies involved in Healing.

HEALING AND REGENERATION THROUGH COLOUR by Corinne Heline   DeVorss & Co, California, USA. UK distribution Synthesis Publishing. ISBN 0 87516 512 5.
The use of Colour and Music to influence health and promote well being by this extraordinary Clairvoyant.

NEW AGE HEALING by Brenda Johnston, 11 Woodbury Ave. Havant, Hants.
This booklet contains the material of Esoteric Healing study course Part 1.

4. Natural Energies

THE CHAKRAS by C.W. Leadbeater, The Theosophial Publishing House. ISBN 0 8356 0422 5. A description of the body's psychic energy centres by a leading Clairvoyant.

HANDBOOK OF THE AURA by Laneta Gregory and Geoffrey Treissman, Pilgrim Books. ISBN 0946259 13 5. Use of analysis of Auric colours to perceive and forestall major health problems.

NEEDLES OF STONE by Tom Graves, Granada. ISBN 0 586 04965 7. A dowser explores Earth energies and other mysteries.

SACRED GEOMETRY by Nigel Pennick, Turnstone Press. ISBN 085500 127 5. Symbolism and purpose in religious structures.

THE MAGIC OF PRECIOUS STONES by Mellie Uyldert, Turnstone Press. ISBN 0 85500 138 0.
The use of precious stones in religion, magic, astrology and healing.

5. General

PONDER ON THIS, Lucis Press Ltd., London.
A compilation by a student from the writings of Alice A. Bailey and the Tibetan Master D.K.

DEATH: THE GREAT ADVENTURE, Lucis Press Ltd., London.
A compilation by two students from the writings of Alice A. Bailey and the Tibetan Master D.K.

LIFE HERE AND HEREAFTER by Brenda Johnston, 11 Woodbury Avenue, Havant, Hants.
A very helpful booklet for those starting on 'The Path'.

THE TAO OF PHYSICS by Fritjof Capra, Fontana/Collins. ISBN 0 00 635707 5.
Parallels between subatomic physics and eastern mysticism.

KNOWLEDGE OF THE HIGHER WORLDS AND ITS ATTAINMENT by Rudolf Steiner, The Rudolph Steiner Press. ISBN 910142 20 3.
Presents the means whereby everyone can develop knowledge of a world of Soul and Spirit.

EDUCATING AS AN ART edited by E. Piening & Nick Lyons, Rudolf Steiner Press.
Essays on the Rudolf Steiner Method: Waldorf Education.

Index